Staging **Harriet's House**

critical qualitative research

CRITICAL ISSUES FOR LEARNING AND TEACHING

Shirley R. Steinberg and Gaile S. Cannella
Series Editors

Vol. 7

The Critical Qualitative Research series
is part of the Peter Lang Education list.
Every volume is peer reviewed and meets
the highest quality standards for content and production.

PETER LANG
New York • Washington, D.C./Baltimore • Bern
Frankfurt • Berlin • Brussels • Vienna • Oxford

Tara Goldstein

Staging Harriet's House

Writing and Producing Research-Informed Theatre

PETER LANG
New York • Washington, D.C./Baltimore • Bern
Frankfurt • Berlin • Brussels • Vienna • Oxford

Library of Congress Cataloging-in-Publication Data

Goldstein, Tara.
Staging Harriet's house: writing and producing
research-informed theatre / Tara Goldstein.
p. cm. — (Critical qualitative research; v. 7)
Includes bibliographical references and index.
1. Goldstein, Tara—Harriet's house.
2. Goldstein, Tara—Dramatic production.
3. Lesbian theater—Production and direction—Canada. I. Title.
PR9199.4.G65S73 812'.6—dc23 2011031004
ISBN 978-1-4331-1403-8 (paperback)
ISBN 978-1-4331-1404-5 (hardcover)
ISBN 978-1-4539-0185-4 (e-book)
ISSN 1947-5993

Bibliographic information published by **Die Deutsche Nationalbibliothek**
Die Deutsche Nationalbibliothek lists this publication in the "Deutsche Nationalbibliografie"; detailed bibliographic data is available on the Internet at http://dnb.d-nb.de/.

Cover art by Lisa Rupchand.

The paper in this book meets the guidelines for permanence and durability of the Committee on Production Guidelines for Book Longevity of the Council of Library Resources.

29 Broadway, 18th floor, New York, NY 10006
www.peterlang.com

Printed in the United States of America

To Margot, who among many other things, drove the cargo van in forty-degree heat on the day we struck the set.

CONTENTS

ACKNOWLEDGMENTS

This book about writing and producing *Harriet's House* was undertaken with the strong support of an incredibly smart, creative and generous network of people. I owe them all a great deal of thanks.

First, I want to thank and acknowledge the participants I interviewed for the *Harriet's House* project and the writers and filmmakers of the texts I worked with during the research and writing phase of *Harriet's House*. Their perspectives appear in the script and in this book. I also want to acknowledge Amy Gullage, Monica Nunes, Dan Parker, and Manu Sharma for their research and production assistance. The Social Sciences and Humanities Research Council of Canada funded the research first, through its Small Institutional Grants program, then through its Standard Research Grant program. The Department of Curriculum, Teaching and Learning at the Ontario Institute for Studies in Education (OISE), University of Toronto provided institutional support of the project.

Next, I have benefited greatly from the instruction and support of my writing instructors and colleagues at Gotham Writing Workshop, Spalding University, the Prince Edward Island Conservatory, and the Moving Pen writing group. While my writing instructors are named in the book, most of my colleagues are not. However, I would like them to know that their feedback and friendship during our writing sessions have been important to me. I especially want to acknowledge and thank Tanya Lewis and the late Sharon Rosenberg, the members of my first writing group, which began in the mid-1990s. With the initial support of Toronto writer Ann Decter, Tanya, Sharon and I wrote together for nine years. Our friendship and mutual encouragement in the early years of writing and building an academic career at the University of Toronto helped me to develop the skills that made the writing and producing *Harriet's House* possible. Likewise the love, support, and excellent editorial eye Margot Huycke has offered in the fifteen years we have been together has been central to creating a writing life.

It takes many people to support a project like *Harriet's House*. I want to thank and acknowledge all the members of the creative teams who worked on the *Harriet's House* project. My brothers Carl Goldstein and Richard Goldstein provided much-needed publicity and financial support for the production. Thanks and appreciation also go out to the Warden of Hart House, Louise Cowin, who hosted the opening night reception, and to the team from Hart House Theatre. Finally, I want to give a heartfelt thank you to the production's sponsors and patrons; the audience members who came to see the play; my Lowitz, Goldstein, and Huycke families; Karen Kaffko, and my colleagues and friends from OISE, the University of Toronto, and the Toronto District School Board.

I wrote this book while on sabbatical in Broadbeach, Australia. Both Bebe Rupchand and Amy Gullage at the Ontario Institute for Studies in Education sent reference material from Toronto to Broachbeach. I want to thank them for their support.

Feedback on early drafts of this book came from Margot Huycke, Shirley Steinberg, Catherine Doherty, Amy Gullage and Jocelyn Wickett. Your generous feedback helped me deepen, layer and sharpen the story of writing and producing *Harriet's House*.

Finally, I want to acknowledge and thank the staff at Peter Lang who published *Staging Harriet's House:* Shirley Steinberg, the Series Editor; Sophie Appel, Design and Production Supervisor; Catherine Tung, and Chris Myers, Acquiring Editor. Your expertise has been very much appreciated.

My love for the theatre began early on when my grandmother Rose Roback Goldstein took me to both English and French children's theatre in Montréal, and enrolled me in children's theatre classes run by Dorothy Davis and Violet Walters. The work of *Harriet's House* both on the stage and in the classroom holds her passion for people, storytelling and social justice. She would have loved to see it. And I would have loved her to see it.

PREFACE

Harriet's House at Hart House Theatre

In the summer of 2010, I produced my play *Harriet's House* as part of the annual Toronto Pride Festival. The project had been in the works for two years, and when I began planning for the production, I didn't know that Toronto would be hosting the 2010 G20 summit. The annual summit brings together world leaders to discuss ways of promoting worldwide financial stability and sustainable economic growth and development. In preparation for the Toronto summit, a steel fence was built around the centre of the city to create a security zone that would protect G20 participants in the event that any of the planned protest rallies by anti-poverty, environmental and women's reproductive rights activists "got out of hand." All protest activities were limited to Queen's Park, which was some distance away from the summit meetings.

Located right beside Queen's Park, the University of Toronto also prepared for the G20 summit. *Harriet's House* was booked to play at Hart House Theatre, one of several theatres located at the University of Toronto, the same weekend as the G20 summit. Fearing that there might be violence at the protest site, the University of Toronto decided to shut down during the G20 meetings. On Friday evening of the May 24th long weekend, four weeks into rehearsal and four weeks before opening night, I received an e-mail from Louise Cowin, the Warden of

Hart House and a good friend and colleague, telling me that I would have to find another venue or pick another weekend to stage the show.

Harriet's House had been conceptualized, funded and promoted as an official Pride event from the inception of the project. With the University of Toronto closing over the opening weekend of the Pride Festival, the show had to be rescheduled for the closing weekend. But rescheduling the production wasn't ideal. It meant putting the show on during the July 1st long weekend, a weekend when many members of our audience would be out of town. It also meant placing the show in competition with the first week of the Toronto Fringe Festival. One hundred and fifty other theatre productions would be trying to attract the same audience members and theatre critics we hoped to draw in for *Harriet's House*. Finally, re-scheduling the production meant competing with the free Cindi Lauper concert that was playing in Queen's Park on Saturday night as part of the Pride Festival. Rescheduling also meant changing the posters and flyers that the company had been distributing for weeks, exchanging the tickets that had been bought in advance, and confirming that all the actors were available to perform during the July 1st weekend. Postponing the production by a week was going to be difficult and risky. But director Jocelyn Wickett and I decided to do it anyway. We moved forward step by step, and in the end attracted 450 people to the three performances we staged at Hart House Theatre.

This book tells a set of stories of how I wrote and produced *Harriet's House*, a research-informed play about transnational adoption in a same-sex family, for the 2010 Toronto Pride Festival. In doing so, it offers some practical advice to others who want to write and produce research-informed theatre. The book begins with a story of how I became part of the world of research-informed playwriting and why researchers, playwrights and theatre artists choose to write and stage research-informed theatre. It then moves on to a set of stories of how I wrote and workshopped the play, found a venue, put together an artistic team, created a budget, pursued funding, publicized the production, and assessed the quality of the project. In writing about research-informed theatre, I draw on the experiences of other writers and theatre artists as well as my own. Readers will find references to work by American, Australian, British, and other Canadian research-informed theatre artists. The last chapter of the book lists ten questions I have been asked about *Harriet's* House, research-informed theatre and arts-based research, and provides answers to these questions. This last chapter is followed by three appendices that include a copy of the performance script, biographies of the artistic team and a selected bibliography on research-informed theatre for readers who would like to read more.

· 1 ·

THE WORLD OF RESEARCH-INFORMED THEATRE

The world of research-informed theatre attracts a variety of people from different backgrounds. Research-informed theatre artists include playwrights who are looking for ways to investigate a particular aspect of the human condition or a particular moment of human history that can be dramatized and performed for an audience. They also include academic researchers working in a variety of fields—including anthropology, sociology, psychology, education, health care, women's studies, justice studies, ethnic studies, cultural studies, political science, journalism, human communication and performance studies—who are looking for an effective way of sharing their research findings with audiences both within and outside of the academy.[1] I am both. A playwright and an academic.

I wrote my first research-informed play, *Hong Kong, Canada*,[2] in the late 1990s as an early-mid-career academic who had been formally trained in an anthropological research method known as critical ethnography. While the work of ethnography is to describe a culture or a way of life from the point of view of those who are living it, critical ethnography attempts to get beyond people's daily assimilated experience to expose the ways in which structures of power reproduce themselves in everyday life.

For the first twelve years of my academic life, I engaged in traditional critical ethnographic research in the field of education. I undertook two critical ethnographic studies on the topic of teaching and learning in multilingual, multicultural, and multiracial classrooms. The first focused on teaching English as a Second Language to women working in a bilingual Portuguese and English toy factory (*Two Languages at Work: Bilingual Life on the Production Floor*) and the second on teaching and learning in a bilingual Cantonese and English high school (*Teaching and Learning in Multilingual School: Choices, Risks and Dilemmas*).[3] However, in the late nineties, I began to experiment with turning the findings of my ethnographic research into a play script that could be read aloud by a group of participants or performed before audiences. I called my work "performed ethnography," and soon learned that what I was writing was also known as "performance ethnography" and "ethnodrama."

The term "performance ethnography" has been used by sociologist Norman Denzin to refer to performances that ethnographers stage from their interviews and observation field notes.[4] The term "ethnodrama" has been used by researcher and theatre artist Johnny Saldaña. He describes an ethnodrama as consisting of a dramatic script that includes significant selections of narrative that have been collected through interviews, observation field notes, journal entries, diaries, media articles and court proceedings.[5] For Saldaña, ethnodrama is different from "ethnotheatre," which uses the traditional craft and artistic techniques of theatre production to mount a live performance event of research participants' experiences and/or a researcher's interpretation of data. In ethnotheatre, the fieldwork conducted by a researcher is preparation for a theatrical production.

Like Saldaña, health researcher/playwrights Jim Mienczakowski and Teresa Moore believe that ethnodrama is different from traditional theatrical work. They describe it as a new aesthetic that values the accurate interpretation of research findings over the style, mode, and traditions of theatrical presentation.[6] For example, Mienczakowski's ethnodrama *Busting: The Challenge of the Drought Spirit* is a "documentary-style presentation" of the experiences of health workers in a detoxification centre that lets the data "do the talking."[7] For Mienczakowski, the audiences for his ethnodrama work are often comprised of those with a close relationship to or lived experience of the themes of the piece. Their anticipation of performance and entertainment are secondary to their expectations of theatrical engagement.

The performance is a shared context that actors and audience members co-construct, through which they connect because of their own emotional links to the topic of the research/performance.

The literary turn in American anthropology

My own experimentation with performed ethnography was a deliberate attempt to engage with the "literary turn" in American anthropology that had begun in the mid-1980s. This turn was set off by discussions about the predicaments of cultural representation in ethnography raised in the 1986 anthology *Writing Culture: The Poetics and Politics of Ethnography*. The anthology was edited by James Clifford, a historian of anthropology, and George Marcus, an anthropologist and critic of "realist" traditions in ethnographic writing.[8] As explained by feminist anthropologist Ruth Behar, the book's purpose was to make an incredibly obvious point: anthropologists write. The ethnographies they write—"a strange cross between the realist novel, the travel account, the memoir, and the scientific report"—had to be understood in terms of poetics and politics.[9]

At the heart of the literary turn in American anthropology was the understanding that ethnographers *invent* rather than represent ethnographic truths.[10] Ethnographies were not the transparent mirrors of culture that traditionally trained realist ethnographers presumed them to be. The contributors of *Writing Culture* questioned the politics of a poetics, that is, a system of writing, which relied on the words and stories of (frequently less privileged) others for its existence, without providing any of the benefits of authorship to the research participants who assisted the anthropologist in the writing of their culture.

In response to these predicaments of cultural representation, James Clifford set out a new agenda for American anthropology in his introduction to *Writing Culture*: Anthropology needed to encourage more innovative, dialogic, and experimental writing that highlighted the ways in which ethnographies are invented by the ethnographers who write them. At the same time, the "new ethnography" needed to reflect a more profound self-consciousness of the workings of power and the partialness of all truth, both in the text and in the world. As summarized by Ruth Behar, while the new ethnography would not resolve the profoundly troubling issues of inequality in a world fueled by global capitalism,"[11] it could at least attempt to decolonize the power relations inherent in the presentation of "Other people."[12]

Crossing the border between anthropology and theatre

The playwright who first inspired me to experiment with new ethnographic writing and cross the border between anthropology and theatre was anthropologist Dorinne Kondo. I was introduced to Kondo's ethnographic play *Dis(graceful) Conduct* in Ruth Behar and Deborah Gordon's 1995 anthology *Women Writing Culture*.[13] The anthology set out to trace a women's literary tradition in American anthropology. This was a tradition that was notably absent from Clifford and Marcus' anthology, which did not include any writing by women anthropologists. *Dis(grace)ful Conduct* is a dramatic commentary about Orientalism and the harassment of Asian women, written in the form of a comedy/musical.[14]

My first play, *Hong Kong, Canada*, was created from the findings of my second critical ethnographic study on bilingual school life. While I used realist ethnographic methods to collect and analyze the data from the study, and shared my findings in academic journals and edited books, I also blended realist, interpretive, and dramatic techniques to construct an ethnographic play that could be read aloud and discussed by my students who were studying to become teachers.

American sociologists and writers on qualitative research methodology Yvonne Lincoln and Laurel Richardson have written about the importance of producing multiple texts in contemporary postmodern times. Richardson argues that at the core of postmodernism is the *doubt* that any method or theory, discourse or genre, tradition or novelty can claim to present the whole truth. Yet, a postmodern position "does allow us to know 'something' without claiming to know everything. Having a partial, local, historical [situated] knowledge is still knowing."[15]

Lincoln works with this idea of partial knowledge and suggests that if all texts are only partial and historically and culturally situated, then there is only a limited value to presenting the multiple understandings that come from an ethnographic project in a single text. Contemporary ethnographers, she believes, need to create multiple texts, each of which speaks to a different audience.[16]

My journal articles and book chapters on bilingual school life have been written for researchers and academics interested in issues of multilingualism in schooling, and authorize themselves through the citation of other scholarly texts. The play, however, has been written for teachers negotiating linguistic, cultural and racial differences in their classrooms and schools. Readings and performances of the play authorize themselves through their ability to evoke and invoke shared emotional experience and understanding between the performers and the audience. Several years after writing *Hong Kong, Canada* I brought this blend of realist, interpretative and dramatic research and writing techniques to the *Harriet's House* project. The fictional characters in *Harriet's House* experience the same conflicts and dilemmas as the participants in my interviews and the families in the personal narratives and documentary films I researched. A methodological account of how I researched and wrote *Harriet's House* can be found in chapter two. In chapter three, I provide a reflective assessment of my methodological work.

Further reading outside the discipline of anthropology took me into the world of theatre and led me to the works of American playwrights Eve Ensler (*The Vagina Monologues*), Moisés Kaufman (*The Laramie Project*) and Anna Deavere Smith (*Fires in the Mirror* and *Twilight, Los Angeles 1992*), who were crossing the border between theatre-making and anthropology as theatre artists. Each of these artists made use of dramatic monologues to tell important research stories.

Eve Ensler and *The Vagina Monologues*

The Vagina Monologues, written in 1998, evolved from Ensler's conversations and interviews with over 200 women about their vaginas.[17] The play was written as a set of monologues that include near-verbatim interview texts, composite interviews, as well as original pieces that were inspired by the interviews. None of the monologues is assigned to a particular character. Each is performed as an individual piece that could be spoken by any woman. The play resonated with a great number of women and is now staged annually on university campuses around the world on "V-Day," as a fundraising event to support projects working to challenge and end violence against women.

Moisés Kaufman and *The Laramie Project*

The Laramie Project, an American "docudrama" written and performed by Moisés Kaufman and the Tectonic Theatre Company in 2001 tells the story of the murder of Matthew Shepard.[18] In 1998 Shepard, a twenty-one-year-old gay student studying at the University of Wyoming in Laramie, was tied to a cattle fence, beaten, robbed and left to die. He was accidentally discovered eighteen hours later by a biker, who alerted the police. Ambulances were dispatched and Shepard was taken to a local hospital, but never regained consciousness. He died several days later due to head injuries, and two local young men were charged with murder. Kaufman and the Tectonic Theatre Company interviewed people who lived in Laramie to capture the emotions and reactions of the people who were most affected by the crime. The play is based on more than four hundred interviews with about one hundred Laramie residents, as well as journal entries written by Kaufman and the members of Tectonic Theater Project that reflect their own reactions to the murder and to the interviews they carried out.

Structured as a documentary, each character in the play represents one of the people who was interviewed. The play re-enacts the story of Matthew Shepard's murder through a set of verbatim monologues based on those interviews. Some of the characters represent the members of the company themselves. Their monologues, based on journal entries they wrote during their fieldwork, describe what it felt like to be working in Laramie and talking to people about what happened to Matthew Shepard. The purpose of the project was to explore Laramie's response to the crime. A larger question for Tectonic Theatre Company became what this crime revealed not just about Laramie, but also about American culture in general.

Ten years after the murder, the Tectonic Theatre Company returned to Laramie to conduct new interviews with the people to whom they had spoken during the first project. The purpose of this second project was to examine what had changed in Laramie in the decade since the murder. The interviews were used to create a follow-up play called *The Laramie Project: Ten Years Later*. On October 12, 2009, American theatres in all fifty states presented a reading of *The Laramie Project: Ten Years Later*. This national reading provided an opportunity for audiences across the United States to explore the issues raised by the play simultaneously. My friend and colleague Jeanne Haggard from Spalding University directed the stage reading at Texas Tech University in Lubbock, where she is completing a doctorate degree in the Fine Arts program. In her blog entries about her experience directing *Ten Years Later*, Jeanne writes:

> It was so humbling to know that we were reading the script at the same time Tectonic was reading it in New York, and [that] other theatres, universities, and high schools were also reading it all across the world. We were connected to the live pre-show feed from NY and saw Glenn Close, Judy Shepard [Matthew's mother], and Moisés Kaufman. Then everyone did their reading and hooked back up with NY after for the post-show discussion. All in all it was very exciting to be a part of theatre history because Tectonic accomplished something that had never been done in live theatre before. There were 150 locations participating in this event. It still gives me chills thinking about it—we rocked!

Anna Deavere Smith and *Twilight: Los Angeles 1992*

Like *The Laramie Project*, Anna Deavere Smith's projects *Fires in the Mirror* and *Twilight, Los Angeles 1992* respond to a moment of violence in contemporary American history.[19] Both pieces are part of a larger project entitled *On the Road: A Search for American Character*, which began in 1983. *Fires in the Mirror* examines the violence that broke out in Brooklyn, New York, after a rabbi's motorcade ran over and killed an African-American boy. A Jewish student visiting from Australia was killed in retaliation. Smith interviewed bystanders, community members and leaders about the incidents, and then performed as each of them in a solo performance, shifting from one character to another by removing a hat, putting on glasses and changing her accent.

Twilight: Los Angeles 1992 focuses on the violence that took place in Los Angeles following the verdict in the first Rodney King trial. Rodney King is an African American man who was severely beaten by four white Los Angeles policemen after he was stopped for speeding in 1991. When the officers charged with the beating were found innocent (except for one charge against one of the officers for excessive use of force), there was an explosive reaction in South Central Los Angeles. A peaceful protest rally at a church broke into violence involving shootings, beatings, and looting. Some of the vandalism led to arson, and engulfed a large section of South Central Los Angeles in fire. Smith interviewed a wide range of people about the beating, trial, and subsequent violence. She then edited and arranged parts of these interviews into monologues, and once again performed all of the characters.

Unlike *The Laramie Project*, Smith's performance piece doesn't have a storyline. The monologues are juxtaposed to highlight the multiple viewpoints expressed in the interviews. From about one hundred and seventy-five interviews she conducted for the project, Smith presents between twenty-five and forty-five characters in each performance, depending on her production venue.[20] To remind her audiences and readers of the issues, Smith provides a chronological "Time Line" in her production playbills of the important events referenced in the piece. The time line is what provides the story.

Like *The Laramie Project*, the characters in the piece are all people Smith interviewed. They include Daryl F. Gates, the white Chief of the Los Angeles Police Department (LAPD) at the time of the beating; Angela King, Rodney King's aunt who is seeking justice for the beating of her nephew; Sergeant Charles Duke, a white member of the LAPD Special Weapons and Tactical Unit who was a defense witness in the trials of the officers who beat Rodney King (a second trial held after the first trial was deemed to be a mistrial); an unnamed white juror in the first trial, who breaks into tears as he recalls his ambivalent feelings about the verdict and its aftermath; Maxine Waters, an African-American congresswoman who was representing South Central Los Angeles at the time of the trial, and Cornel West, an African American scholar who compares the violent reaction to the verdict to the "gangsterous orientation" in Sylvester Stallone's *Rambo* character movies and rap music. In an introduction to the published piece, Smith writes that her intention was not to place blame for what happened in South Central Los Angeles, but to document a critical, violent moment in American race relations and to help the process of healing by sharing many different viewpoints about what happened.[21] Such an intention is a good example of the desires and purposes behind many research-informed theatre projects: to raise awareness, propose alternatives, provide healing, and inspire change.

Ensler, Kaufman and Smith's work with monologues has informed the writing of each of my plays, all of which contain at least one monologue that tells of an important moment in a character's life. These moments speak to significant research themes in the play, such as the pain of speaking English in *Hong Kong, Canada*; the challenge of coming out in a religious family and community in *Snakes and Ladders*, and the impact of anti-Semitism on everyday life in *Lost Daughter*.

Learning to write drama

To begin learning how to write plays that could dramatize my research findings in the ways that Ensler, Kaufman and Smith did, I signed up for a ten-week on-line playwriting course with an organization called the Gotham Writing Workshop.[22] Each week, I was sent an on-line lecture about an important aspect of playwriting (for example, what to think about when creating the world of your play), and an assignment that gave me the opportunity to practice what was discussed in the lecture. Laurence Carr, my first Gotham writing instructor, sent me back some brief feedback on each of my assignments, which helped me see how my work could be improved. In addition to the weekly assignment, there was a weekly on-line discussion on the lecture that my classmates and I could join. Three times during the ten-week course, I was invited to submit a scene from my play-in-progress and receive feedback from my classmates, as well as from my instructor, Laurence. I took the course twice in order to complete a first draft of *Hong Kong, Canada*. To move from a first draft to a second draft of the script, I enrolled in Gotham's "script doctor" program, which allowed me to work one-on-one with Laurence. The script continued to develop when I worked with director Tammy Chan and a group of my teacher education students at OISE to rehearse for a first reading of the play.

The introductory playwriting course offered by Laurence focused on the dramatic form of naturalism (also known as realism). I learned how to write a play that featured a unified storyline, psychologically plausible characters and emotional engagement—hallmarks of conventional mainstream theatre writing and production. Since one of the reasons I wanted to learn how to write ethnographic plays was to engage mainstream school teachers in social and political issues related to schooling, learning to write conventional naturalistic/realist drama was a good first step.

In her book about the contemporary political theatre in Australia, *Power Plays: Australian Theatre and the Public Agenda*, theatre scholar Hilary Glow argues that mainstream theatre can be a powerful space for playwrights who want to engage the public in discussion of current political events.[23] She profiles the work of eight contemporary Australian playwrights, all who see theatre as a place for public political engagement, and all who choose to write within the conventional, mainstream form of naturalistic/realist theatre. Asking why political playwrights might choose to write for the mainstream, Glow turns to American theatre scholar Alisa Solomon, who suggests it is because the theatre-going public—largely college-educated and middle-class—are among the people who most consistently vote, most frequently write to their congresspeople, and most reliably engage in local civic activities.[24] The playwrights Glow profiles echo this sentiment; they have chosen to work within the framework of mainstream theatre to reach a wide audience.

My work with *Hong Kong, Canada* showed me that ethnographic playwriting offered me a productive way of both responding to the dilemmas discussed by postmodern anthropologists, and sharing my research findings with teachers. The play, which presented conflicts documented in my fieldwork through a storyline and characters that were fictional, allowed me to remind readers that ethnographers invent rather than represent ethnographic truths. As well, by hosting a reading of an early draft of *Hong Kong, Canada* I could invite my research participants to read the play and tell me whether or not my understandings and analysis of the issues in their school resonated with them. Working with my participants' feedback, I was able to rewrite my script, and work towards ensuring that what was being presented was typical of their experiences. Furthermore, as my students began reading aloud and discussing *Hong Kong, Canada* with one another in my teacher education classes, I began to recognize the pedagogical power of performed ethnography.

Teaching with *Hong Kong, Canada*

Hong Kong, Canada is a play about the language issues and dilemmas facing Canadian immigrant high school students from Hong Kong. Set in a fictional school in Toronto, the play tells the story of Wendy Chan, the assistant editor of the student newspaper, as she struggles with the fallout of having published a controversial issue. Wendy is a recent immigrant from Hong Kong in a school where more than one-third of the student population speaks Cantonese as their primary language. Sam Tsang, the advertising manager of the newspaper, is also from Hong Kong. Joshua Greenberg, the white Jewish editor of the newspaper, is Wendy's love interest.

Joshua, Wendy and Sam face two challenges: they must reduce the newspaper's debt and get more students to read the paper. Joshua searches for a controversial issue to write about, and finds one when his friend Sarah complains about Chinese students singing in Cantonese at talent night. When Wendy agrees to write a related article on why she only speaks English at school, she and Sam fight about the impact her column might have on Cantonese-speakers at the school. A few nights later, as Wendy and Sam are laying-out the newspaper for publication, Sam informs Wendy that he has sold ten ads to customers who want to advertise tutoring services for Cantonese-speaking students at the school. The ads are written in Chinese. At first Wendy doesn't want to publish the ads, but under pressure from Sam, she decides to include them in the paper. The publication of the Chinese ads provokes Sarah into starting a petition for an English-only policy at school. In response, the principal asks Ms. Diamond, one of the English teachers, to run a school hearing so that she can get further student input on the issue. The hearing and the play end with Ms. Diamond telling the students that she will give the principal a report on what was said at the hearing. The issue of implementing an English-only policy at the school remains unresolved.

Hong Kong, Canada: Excerpt From Scene 16

Sarah: I strongly support the idea of an English-only policy at Trudeau. A lot of people were mad about how much Chinese was used at Talent Night. As Joshua Greenberg said in his editorial, "If it is not possible to obtain performers in each and every language represented in our school, then only English should be used because it's the language that we all have in common."

Rita: I am East Indian. It would have been great if one or two Bengali songs had been performed at Talent Night. But we didn't go for it. Why should we stop those who went for it?

Joshua: Because people feel left out when people speak Cantonese and they can't understand them. Instead of promoting multiculturalism at our school, the event divided us. That wouldn't have happened if—

Sam: *(Interrupting)* It was Talent Night, not English night. We were there to watch people perform and demonstrate their talent. You can enjoy a performance without understanding every word. It happens at heavy metal concerts all the time.

Sarah: An English-only policy would ensure that when I go to a school event, I would be able to understand every single word that is spoken.

Sam: People who are uncomfortable when they don't understand Chinese are not used to sharing space with people who speak different languages. They want to take away other people's rights so that they don't have to feel uncomfortable, not even for a moment. That's not fair. Toronto—

Sarah: *(Interrupting)* If all acts at Talent Night had been performed in English, it would have assisted those who are learning the language to—

Sam: *(Interrupting)* But Toronto is no longer just an English-speaking city. You have to share space with people who speak languages you don't understand. We all have to share the discomfort.

Joshua: It's good for people to be forced to speak English at school. They'll learn it faster. Look at Wendy Chan—

Rita: *(Interrupting)* Instead of an English-only policy, we should be offering Cantonese classes during the school day and encouraging as many students as possible to take them. There would be a lot less anger if more people could speak Cantonese.

Joshua: An English-only policy will benefit our Chinese students in the long run. It's good thing.

Rita: Maybe we should be thinking of making Cantonese classes compulsory for students in this school.

Ms. Diamond: *(Scribbling a last few notes)* Thank you all for your contributions. Our last speaker this afternoon is Wendy Chan. Wendy?

Wendy: *(Stepping forward)* The day after they enrolled me at Trudeau my father and mother left Toronto to go back to Hong Kong. The last words my mother said to me as she went through security gate at the airport were "I want you to speak English." *(In Cantonese)* ["You have to learn to speak English well"] *(In English)* My mother wanted all the advantages that were available to Canadian-born students to be available to me. To please her, I decided I would only speak English in school. And speaking English all day did open some doors. I had enough confidence to go on Mr. Wilson's camping trip even though I had never gone camping before and didn't know anyone else who had signed up for the trip. And on that

> trip I met people who were born here and one or two became important friends for a while. But choosing to only speak English also closed some doors. I didn't make any friends with people from Hong Kong. *(In Cantonese)* ["They thought I wasn't interested in being friends because I always spoke English."] *(In English)* They thought I was Canadian-born, *juk-sin*, a banana, white-washed. I miss speaking Cantonese. My mother doesn't know how to hard it is to speak English all day, everyday. She is in Hong Kong where she can speak Cantonese. Some days my mouth, my cheeks, my lips hurt. When my mother tells me, "I want you to speak English" she thinks only of the doors that might open. Not the doors that close. An English-only policy will close doors for those of us who speak other languages. Unable to say what we would like to say in English, some of us will stay silent. An English-only policy also closes doors for those of us who want to practice speaking other languages with students who already know them well. In the last few weeks, I have learned that the doors we have opened are sometimes slammed shut by an unexpected force. It is prudent to keep as many doors open as possible. Thank you.

The first time I taught with *Hong Kong, Canada*, a group of my teacher education students performed the play for the rest of their classmates. The performance of the play was constructed as an assignment. Working with Hong Kong-born, Cantonese-speaking director Tammy Chan, my students prepared a polished reading of the play for their classmates and gave an oral presentation of what they had learned from rehearsing and performing the play. The performers also produced a written reflection of what they had learned about teaching students from different linguistic, cultural and racial backgrounds through their involvement with the performance. The reflections the students wrote demonstrated that they had learned quite a bit and I wrote an article for *Teaching Education Journal* on what performed ethnography had to offer to anti-racist teacher education.[25] Here are several excerpts from my students' reflection pieces on their work with *Hong Kong, Canada*, and my own comments on what they had say.

Reflection by the student playing the role of Joshua

> . . . It is evident to me that Josh has never really thought about the use of language in school before, probably because he has never had to. Being white and male, one takes things for granted . . . Josh has probably never had to worry about being able to understand the teacher or other kids at school. Also, he has probably never had to worry about fitting in with the other people in his community because of the language he speaks . . .

The student who played the role of Joshua talks about his character having the privilege of not having to worry about being able to understand the teacher or other kids at school. He also links the idea of linguistic privilege to white privilege, which was a notion we had discussed in our course.[26] This tells me that the conflicts and characterizations in the play can provoke discussion around linguistic privilege, especially if some work around privilege has already taken place. Many of my students are monolingual English speakers. Like Joshua, they do not have any experience of having to "do school" in a language they are not proficient in. Nor have they experienced what it's like to have to decide which language to speak at school. The characters of Wendy and Sam provide them with an opportunity to witness the experience of those who do.

Reflection by the student playing Wendy

> . . . The issue of "acting white" when speaking English is also dealt with in the play. Sam accuses Wendy of speaking English to "act white" in order to be with Joshua. This reminds me of a poem called "Speak White" written by Quebecois, Michelle Lalonde in the 1960s. The theme of the poem is maintaining dignity . . .
>
> . . . "Speak white" is repeated 16 times in the entire poem and with each time the tone seemed to get angrier. It is implied that speaking white is speaking English. The poem also emphasizes the difference in culture between the English- and French-speaking Canadians, and speaking "white" is like denying the French culture. The poem ends off by saying "we are not alone," meaning that they are not the only cultural group that has felt oppressed and that there is strength in their numbers. This relates to schools where students who find it difficult to express thoughts in a second language feel that they are being forced to comply with the culture of dominance. They may develop negative, angry attitudes towards teachers and education . . . In the play, Sam's response to the language issues are through anger . . .

The student playing Wendy reflects on the phrase "acting white" (used by Sam in an argument with Wendy over an article about her decision to only use English in school). In her analysis, the student argues that speaking and acting white means speaking and acting English. Here, she is able to describe the way the dominance of whiteness and English intersect to produce a culture of dominance that some high school students feel "forced to comply with." This sophisticated analysis is then linked to a discussion of anger that some students feel in response to their experience with the culture of dominance.

It is the anger that is attached to Sam's accusation that helps make the phrase "acting white" memorable for the student playing Wendy. After all, that anger was directed at her during the performance of the play. In moving from writing realist ethnography to writing ethnographic plays, I have been able to move from an activity of representation to an activity which sociologist Carolyn Ellis calls "evocation."[27] An evocative and dramatic story shows interaction in a way that allows the performer and spectator to participate more fully in the emotional process of resolving conflicts. Performers and spectators are not merely observers of the resolution of the conflicts in the story, they become participants. It is possible to use the power of emotion to help teacher education students write focused reflection pieces on what they have learned about teaching across linguistic and racial difference through their engagement with the play.

Reflection by the students playing Sarah and Sam

> . . . I was often wondering what I would have done (as a future English teacher) had I been petitioned for an English-only policy by a fair number of students. As much as I believe that there needs to be flexibility and definitely an increase in the education of teachers on how immigrant children feel, I still also believe that within the English classroom, English should be practiced and spoken. As for ESL classrooms, I believe it is extremely important for the students to at least attempt to speak English with each other in the classroom (for practice), but reverting to their first-language *should be allowed* in extreme cases of difficulty in expression or comprehension.
>
> . . . The more I read the play the more difficult I found it was to come up with a solution that would make everyone happy. In a way, I believe that letting students speak another language other than English will make them feel more at ease at the school, and will thus make them feel more at ease in learning English. On the other hand, I think that sometimes allowing students to speak languages other than English in Toronto schools can hinder English learning and school spirit.

The students playing the roles of Sarah and Sam discuss the complexity of the dilemmas faced by the students and principal of the school featured in the play and articulate their own struggles with the contradictory beliefs they hold on whether or not multilingual schools should implement English-only policies. The play deliberately concludes in an open-ended way. No solution is provided for the audience. It is up to them to think about the ways principals and teachers might provide leadership around the difficult task of negotiating across linguistic difference. Yet, the teacher-audience also needs leadership from the teacher educator-playwright who has raised such difficult issues. *Hong Kong, Canada* provides my students and me with an opportunity to imagine new anti-racist practices that we have not yet seen modeled in our own work lives. In subsequent readings of the play, I have asked students to write a different ending to the play. In so doing, I treat the play as an "open-text" which can be modified and experimented with. The performance of different endings to *Hong Kong, Canada* provokes rich discussions on ways teachers and principals might move forward.

I was extremely excited with the results of this first reading of *Hong Kong, Canada*, and began to incorporate readings of the play into all of my teacher education classes. I did readings with students in some of my colleagues' classes as well. The readings were set up so that all students had a chance to read a role from the play and engage in a post-reading discussion about the dilemmas presented in the play. I decided to write a second ethnographic play from a critical ethnographic study I was conducting on homophobia and schooling. That play is called *Snakes and Ladders*, and I have had similar success at provoking important discussions on how to challenge homophobia in classrooms and schools through play readings.[28]

Deepening my playwriting skills

While I was in the process of writing *Snakes and Ladders*, I decided to enroll in a Masters of Fine Arts (MFA) program in playwriting at Spalding University in Louisville, Kentucky.[29] I wanted to deepen the playwriting skills I had developed at the Gotham Writing Workshop and become more skilled at using the dramatic conventions other playwrights used. The program at Spalding was a four-semester "brief-residency" program that began with a 10-day residency each semester. Following the residency, each student was matched up with a mentor who was a professional playwright to work on a particular project for the rest of the semester. Every three weeks, students would submit a package of material that the mentors would read and provide feedback on. Being able to complete the degree from home allowed me to continuing working at the University of Toronto while pursuing a MFA degree in Louisville. Attending the residency each semester provided me with a face-to-face community to write and grow with. During the four semesters I spent there, I worked with three mentors—Claudia Johnson, Eric Schmiedl, and Rane Arroyo—and wrote two research-informed plays that I have produced at the Toronto Fringe Festival: *Pound Predators*, which was performed in 2007, and *Lost Daughter*, which was performed in 2008.[30] I also began a series of ten-minute plays about transnational adoption, which ended up providing me with some of the characters for *Harriet's House*. It was a very productive two years. Importantly, completing an MFA program in playwriting helped me to begin to create an identity as a playwright, an identity I could add to my other professional identities: critical ethnographer and teacher educator.

Like my performed ethnographies *Hong Kong, Canada* and *Snakes and Ladders*, *Pound Predators* was written from my own ethnographic research. The play is based on six months of fieldwork I undertook in a Weight Watchers program in 2006, and tells the story of five women "fighting fat" on a program called Pound Predators. By contrast, *Lost Daughter*, a historical drama about anti-Semitism in Toronto is not based on my own research, but on research undertaken by others. As mentioned earlier, *Harriet's House* has been created from personal narratives and documentary films written by and about transnational adoptive and same-sex families, as well as my own interviews with such families. Having broadened my work beyond writing from my own ethnographic research, I now use the term "research-informed theatre" to describe my playwriting. While other research-informed theatre artists have used the term "reality theatre" as an overarching term to describe the verbatim, documentary, and performed ethnography theatre projects described in this chapter, I prefer the term "research-informed theatre."[31] As discussed earlier, my own playwriting work is rooted in the new ethnography of American anthropology, which strives to remind readers that ethnographers invent rather than represent ethnographic truths. Using the term "reality theatre" would distance me from that practice.

While studying at Spalding University, I read work by more playwrights who had conducted research to create theatre projects. For example, I read American Doug Wright's solo play *I Am My Own Wife*, which was based on extensive interviews he had undertaken with Charlotte von Mahlsdorf. Von Mahlsdorf, who died in 2002, lived as a gay transvestite during the Nazi and Communist regimes in East Berlin. The play was developed with Moisés Kaufman and actor Jefferson Mays, who performed almost forty roles in the 2003 Broadway and Off-Broadway productions of the play. I also began to read the work of British playwright Caryl Churchill and American playwright Emily Mann. Each of these playwrights dramatized their research differently, and a brief description of their work illustrates an exciting range of dramatic possibilities for research-informed theatre.

Doug Wright and *I Am My Own Wife*

In structuring his play around Charlotte von Mahlsdorf, Doug Wright made the decision to write himself into the script in the role of narrator so he could represent the story of his research about von Mahlsdorf. The audience accompanies Wright on his research journey, as he attempts to uncover the "truth" of Charlotte's life. He wants to know if the government files he finds match up with the stories Charlotte has told him about her life. By making his own process of research as much a part of the drama as the events in Charlotte's life, Wright is able to highlight the idea that the meaning of an individual life depends on who is telling the story. This idea comes through in the play's subtitle, which is not *The Life of Charlotte von Mahlsdorf*, but *Studies for a Play About the Life of Charlotte von Mahlsdorf*. I have used Wright's approach of writing himself into his script in one of my own plays, *Zero Tolerance*, which is discussed later on in this chapter.

Caryl Churchill and *Top Girls*

Caryl Churchill is an internationally-performed, studied and acclaimed British playwright who has used the writings of political theorists, philosophers and historians in her plays. Churchill's plays explore a wide variety of social topics that dramatize "the anxieties and terrors of contemporary life,"[32] including the ecological crisis, sexual politics, revolution, terror and selfhood. I was introduced to Churchill's work through her 1982 play *Top Girls*.[33]

The play begins with a stand-alone scene of historical and quasi-historical women at a dinner party. The women's dinner party talk is a prelude to a story about the relationship between women and work in 1970s/1980s Britain. *Top Girls* has been discussed in the context of British and North-American second-wave feminism and linked to the goals of feminist historical scholarship, which focused, in part, on bringing the history of women into the historical record.[34] In addition to putting historically remarkable women on stage, *Top Girls* also engages in contemporary debates about what it means for feminists to advocate for fair and equitable treatment in the workplace.

In 1970s Britain these debates were framed around three different feminist positions: liberal/bourgeois; radical/cultural and socialist/materialist. While the liberal feminists focused on the issue of equality between women and men, by fighting for equal pay for equal work, radical feminists emphasized the need to develop women's culture and women's communities. Radical feminists were interested in the question of how women as a group or coalition could build a women-centered socio-political movement based on sisterhood and solidarity among women. In contrast, socialist feminists prioritized the need to address socio-economic inequities among women (and men), arguing that these differences made some women's lived realities more unequal than others. In *Top Girls*, the tensions between the three types of feminist thinking and the lived reality of women's lives in the era of the Thatcher government are portrayed through the juxtaposition of the dinner party scene and the story of three women Marlene, Joyce and Angie.

Marlene runs a London employment agency, which makes her a "top girl." Joyce is Marlene's sister, who has raised Marlene's daughter, Angie, in a run-down section of a seaside town while Marlene has worked her way up at the agency. Churchill examines how material success for a few women does not build solidarity or foster change for the majority. She also explores the personal costs paid by women who have attained the status of "high flyer," a term Marlene uses in the play to describe herself. Many of the women Marlene has assembled at the dinner party only became famous and successful when, like Patient Griselda, they have endured having their children taken from them, or like Pope Joan, when they were able to keep the fact of their pregnancy concealed. As well, while the women at Marlene's dinner party in the first scene intimate a high flyers club of female camaraderie, that first impression is quickly challenged as the women self-obsess, talk over each other, and admit they are miserable.[35] The short scenes in the employment agency that follow the dinner party chart Marlene's career progress at the employment agency. They also chart the difficulty women have supporting each other in a competitive economic climate where any advance of one woman takes something away from another, and where mistrust and lack of understanding creates rifts among women who have made different life choices.[36]

The last part of the play is an extended argument between Joyce, a working-class single mother, and Marlene, a newly middle-class career woman. Their debate takes the play into a discussion of liberal and socialist feminisms. Marlene thinks the country is improving under the leadership of Margaret Thatcher, who is a "tough lady" and "aces" as the first woman prime minister. Joyce argues, "What good's first woman if it's her? I suppose you'd have liked Hitler if he was a woman. Ms. Hitler. Got a lot done, Hitlerina."[37] *Top Girls* engages with ideas from feminist theory and scholarship and brings these ideas to dramatic life. In doing so, the play has been able to stimulate informed talk and public deliberation of how women lived their lives in 1970s/1980s Britain. Almost thirty years later, the play continues to be performed in English-speaking theatres all around the world, provoking discussion of how women live their lives today. Churchill's use of multiple narratives to address different political voices within second wave feminism informed my own use of multiple narratives in *Harriet's House*.

Emily Mann and *The Execution of Justice*

While Doug Wright, like Eve Ensler, Moisés Kaufman and Anna Deavere Smith, used interviews to create *I Am My Own Wife*, Emily Mann used official transcripts of judicial proceedings to create her 1982/1983 play *The Execution of Justice* about the assassination of San Francisco Mayor George Moscone and gay City Supervisor Harvey Milk.[38] The play is based on the transcripts of the trial of Dan White, the politician charged with the murders, as well as on additional interviews with what Mann described as the "uncalled witnesses." These include White's guard, who suggests that White showed absolutely no remorse, and the district attorney, who declares, after the fact, that White was motivated by malice. Tribunal plays like *The Execution of Justice* aim to re-examine official history or re-stage an inquiry so that the audience can "re-view and review" its findings.[39] In the play, the trial itself is on trial in the court of the theatre and is found guilty of a miscarriage of justice. The sentence parallels the actual case, which resulted in White being convicted of a lesser charge of voluntary manslaughter, rather than two counts of first-degree murder, and given a sentence of less than eight years in prison. The play combines live stage action, videos, taped voices and music, and features drag nun and AIDS activist Sister Boom Boom as a voice of consciousness representing human rights for all marginalized people.

Mann's dramatic adaptation of the trial of Dan White inspired the writing of my eighth play, *Zero Tolerance*, which is an adaptation of an investigative report on school safety called *The Road to Health*.[40] The report was commissioned after the shooting of 15-year-old high school student Jordan Manners in the hallway of his Toronto school in May 2007. It was released to the public eight months after the shooting, and one month after its release, I decided to adapt the report into a performance script that could be used to review and provoke discussion about the report's findings and recommendations.

Zero Tolerance

In September 2008, at the beginning of a new school year, eight months after the report was first released, a fourth draft of my script was performed as a staged reading for 500 teacher education students at Ontario Institute for Studies in Education (OISE)'s Safe Schools Conference. The performers included a group of teacher education students, a teacher educator, and three research and development staff members from OISE's Centre for Urban Schooling. The performance was followed by a set of prepared responses from a panel that featured vice-principal and PhD graduate student Dean Barnes from the Halton District School Board, one of OISE's partner school boards; Bev Caswell, an OISE teacher educator; Jeff Kugler, the executive director of the Centre for Urban Schooling and Charis Lo, a teacher education student. Bev, Jeff and Charis had all participated in the staged reading. A further two-hour discussion for audience members wanting to discuss the report in some detail followed the performance. About 30 teacher education students attended. The other students attended workshops on peace-building, conflict resolution, and peer mediation that provided opportunities to discuss practical strategies for dealing with some of the issues raised in the performance.

As I have written in an article published by *Qualitative Inquiry*,[41] adapting the four-volume report into a 30-minute performance for teacher candidates was a challenge. When I began writing the script a month after *The Road to Health* had been released, the report had already begun to be discussed in the local media and in neighbourhood community forums. One of my first adaptation decisions was to include public responses to the report as well as excerpts from the report itself in the performance script. A second decision was imagining the audience that would be engaging with the performance script. OISE's annual Safe Schools Conference for initial teacher education students was an ideal context for a performance of *The Road to Health*, so I decided to write the script for an audience of teacher education students and their teacher educators, who were my colleagues at OISE. These two decisions provided me with several characters for the script: a media reporter and a group of five new teachers. A third decision was to write myself into the script, like Doug Wright, by giving myself the role of narrator. I wanted to remind the audience the performance they were about to see was an interpretation of the report, only one of many that had been made by a number of educators, community leaders, government officials and the media since the report had been released. I also wanted my audience to remember that the performance was inventing truths about the meaning of the report at the same time as it was attempting to represent truths contained in the report. I used the idea of storytelling to do this.

The first scene of *Zero Tolerance*, below, features the opening monologue I wrote for the character Tara Goldstein. The monologue sets up the performance as a story that Goldstein, a playwright and teacher educator from OISE, is telling, based on her reading and understanding of *The Road to Health*. Scene one also demonstrates my use of a screen for projecting images to accompany the performance. The images I have placed in the scene are photographs of the three members of the School Community Safety Advisory Panel who wrote the report. They are human rights lawyer, Julian Falconer; retired teacher, school administrator and Superintendent of Education, Linda MacKinnon and community development worker and administrator, Peggy Edwards. The photographs are a visual reminder that the report itself, along with the recommendations it suggests for creating safer, healthier schools is a document that has been created by three particular individuals. It is also a reminder that the characters in the play are not the individuals portrayed on the screen. They are characters I have created to share excerpts from the report.

Zero Tolerance: Scene 1

GOLDSTEIN: *(To the audience from downstage left)* What do you think of when you hear the words "zero tolerance"? What comes to mind? When I asked a group of my students that question, this is what they said.

TEACHER 1: Bullying.

TEACHER 2: Fighting.

TEACHER 3: Weapons.

TEACHER 4: Suspension.

TEACHER 5: Expulsion.

TEACHER 2: No second chances.

TEACHER 4: Discipline.

TEACHER 5: Safety.

GOLDSTEIN: *(To audience walking from downstage left, to downstage centre, to downstage right)* Is that what you were thinking? Today, I am going to tell you a story about zero tolerance for bad behavior in schools. And how a zero tolerance approach to discipline has not protected students from violence in their schools. My story includes the story of a fifteen-year-old boy named Jordan Manners who was shot in his school during the school day in May 2007. My story also includes excerpts of a report on school safety commissioned by the Director of the Toronto District School Board after the shooting of Jordan Manners. As part of my story, you will hear how some parents, members of the community and the media reacted to the report. You will also hear how some teachers and principals responded. Finally, you'll hear what I think some of what all this may mean for teachers and teacher educators at OISE/UT. *(Walking back to downstage left)* I will begin my story by introducing you to the three people who wrote the report *Road to Health*. Julian Falconer, human rights lawyer.

(FALCONER stands. On the screen is a photo of the real Julian Falconer.)

Peggy Edwards, community worker.

(EDWARDS stands. On the screen is a photo of the real Peggy Edwards.)

Linda McKinnon, retired school teacher.

(MCKINNON stands. On the screen is a photo of the real Linda McKinnon.)

And now I will introduce you to the people who have something to say about the report. A group of pre-service teachers from OISE.

(The TEACHERS stand.)

A principal at the Toronto District School Board.
(The PRINCIPAL stands.)
A group of parents.
(The PARENTS stand.)
A media reporter.
(The REPORTER stands up in the audience, waves and comes downstage left behind TARA GOLDSTEIN.*)*
And last, but certainly not least, a group of high school students at the Toronto District School Board.
(The STUDENTS stand.)
Now that you've met all the characters, let's get on with the story.

Having opened the play with a monologue, I chose to end the piece with a monologue as well. The monologue is followed by the repetition of one single question that closes the play: "How can we do our part?" I intended this final question to serve as a call to action to the audience by their peers on stage.

GOLDSTEIN: And on that note of the need for renewal, my story about zero tolerance and creating safe schools comes to an end. Teachers in Ontario have inherited the consequences of zero tolerance policies and practices and an on-going legacy of racism, sexism, homophobia, classism and other forms of discrimination in schooling. And even though creating safe schools means dealing with matters "beyond academics," there is plenty teachers can do to create healthier learning environments. What are we doing at OISE to help teachers productively respond to discrimination in schools? Are we talking about how to respond to violence against girls? To homophobic bullying? Are teachers learning how to build community in their classrooms? Manage and resolve conflict through communication as well as discipline? Are they learning to develop curriculum that is relevant to their students' lives? What else can teachers be doing? How should they be doing it? How can we do our part at OISE to work against another shooting at a Toronto school? (Pause.) Like Bendale.
TEACHER 1: How can we do our part?
TEACHER 2: How can we do our part?
TEACHER 3: How can we do our part?
TEACHER 4: How can we do our part?
TEACHER 5: How can we do our part?
TEACHERS: How can we do our part?

The call to action for new teachers and teacher educators at OISE to do their part was intended to inspire the audience to take full advantage of the opportunities to learn more about safe school issues and safe school practices at the workshops that immediately followed the performance. For me, doing my part involved adapting *The Road to Health* into a performance piece that allowed 500 new teachers to engage with some of the report's most important findings and recommendations. In writing a play calling on teachers to engage with issues of school safety, I joined other research-informed playwrights who use theatre as a forum for discussing and taking action on pressing social and political issues.

Deepening my playwriting skills

After graduating from the MFA program at Spalding in November 2006, I continued to look out for interesting research-informed theatre projects so I could continue to learn about the different ways playwrights dramatize the research they undertake and how they deal with the ethical issues that emerge in research-informed theatre projects. At the 2009 International Women's Playwright's Conference held in Mumbai, India, I was introduced to Beverley Cooper's Canadian play *Innocence Lost: A Play about Steven Truscott*. The play is based on the story of 14-year-old Steven Truscott's conviction and subsequent acquittal in the murder of his classmate Lynne Harper. Truscott was sentenced to death in 1959, but his death sentence was commuted to life imprisonment. He continued to maintain his innocence until 2007, when his conviction was declared a miscarriage of justice and he was formally acquitted of the crime. Truscott was awarded a $6.5 million compensation package for his wrongful conviction. *Innocence Lost* asks the question of how such a miscarriage of justice could happen.

Beverley Cooper and *Innocence Lost*

When Cooper was commissioned by Blyth Theatre to write the play, she was asked to keep "sensitivity" in mind. Blyth is located in Huron County,where the murder and conviction occurred, and where people's opinions on Truscott's innocence still remained divided. Before writing the play, Cooper talked to people from Huron County to find out why they still thought Truscott was guilty. One of the people she talked to was a son of a deceased juror in the case. He told Cooper that if his father had had the information that led to Truscott's acquittal, he would have found Truscott not guilty. While the play takes a stance that Truscott is innocent, it remains respectful of the fact that some people in Clinton still believe Truscott is guilty. One of the ways that Cooper accomplishes this is by creating a fictional narrator for the play: a thirteen-year-old girl named Sarah who has a crush on Steven Truscott. Cooper uses Sarah to track the changing opinions of the community, which is stunned by the violent death of Lynne Harper. Sarah starts off by defending Steven, insisting that he's "nice" and "shy," until the evidence against him starts mounting. False accounts from witnesses, manipulation of the facts and the lack of credibility from Steven and Lynne's ten- to fourteen-year-old friends, lead most of the residents in Clinton to arrive at one conclusion—Steven Truscott must be guilty. Unlike the judge who presided over Steven's case, Cooper doesn't lead her audience toward a verdict. Sarah's last lines in the play are "It was never going to be black and white. This story was always going to have shades of gray." Cooper's attempt to raise questions about the verdict at the end of play is an excellent example of how research-informed theatre can serve the imperatives of contemporary ethnography. A story with "shades of gray" illustrates how one event can hold multiple perspectives and multiple truths. In *Harriet's House* I have tried to show how the event of Luisa and Ana's adoption means different things to different characters in the play.

Alistair Newton and *The Pastor Phelps Project*

Another interesting Canadian research-informed theatre project is Alistair Newton's *The Pastor Phelps Project: A Fundamentalist Cabaret*. Remounted in 2009 for a University of Toronto conference on homophobia and religion in public schools, the project is about American Calvinist pastor Fred Phelps, leader of a very small Baptist church in Topeka, Kansas. Phelps is well known in the United States for his fire-and-brimstone preaching and for his anti-gay protests. For example, at the funeral of Matthew Shepard, the 21-year-old gay university student featured in *The Laramie Project*, Phelps and the members of his church stood outside the church waving protest signs with slogans like "God hates fags" on them. Newton's project is written as a vaudevillian musical, and its libretto is based on "found text," such as verbatim interviews with church members. Vaudeville was a genre of variety entertainment that was popular in Canada, the United States, Britain and Australia from the early 1880s until the early 1930s. Each performance was made up of a series of separate, unrelated acts grouped together on a common bill, a structure that allows Newton to stage a variety of pieces that satirize different aspects of Phelps's ultra-right Christian fundamentalism. The project also makes use of burlesque, another genre of variety entertainment that involves parody and sometimes grotesque exaggeration. As the program to *The Pastor Phelps Project* announces, the use of burlesque carries part of the play's satirical force:

> Warning! Bible preaching ahead! Pastor Fred Phelps and the good people of the Westboro Baptist Church are here to explain why God hates fags and America is doomed. It's homophobia versus burlesque in a musical cabaret showdown. Stare into the abyss of fundamentalism; sexy political satire with razor wire barbs.

While I haven't worked with the genre of burlesque, I have experimented with the use of parody in my play *Pound Predators*. As mentioned earlier, the play tells the story of five women who are trying to lose weight on a program called "Pound Predators." At the weekly meetings, The Award-Winning Leader works hard to inspire her clients with Pound Predator prizes, weapons of power planning and warnings of sabotage. In a world where women struggle with issues of body size and shape are inundated with aggressive, often humiliating messages about "fighting fat," I use parody to take a different look at losing weight.

Australian verbatim theatre

In closing this discussion of research-informed theatre projects that have inspired and informed my own work, I turn to a recently published anthology on verbatim theatre entitled *Verbatim: Staging Memory and Community*.[42] Edited by Australian playwright Paul Brown, the book is intended for theatre artists, teachers and students who want to create verbatim theatre.

Paul Brown is an academic working in the School of History and Philosophy at the University of New South Wales and is the co-author of *Aftershocks*, a verbatim theatre project about the 1989 earthquake in the Australian city of Newcastle. His book undertakes a detailed examination of five verbatim plays that are part of the New South Wales high school drama curriculum: *The Laramie Project*, discussed earlier; Brown's own play *Aftershock*; *Minefields and Miniskirts*, a play about the experience of Australian women in the Vietnam War, adapted by Terence O'Connell from a book written by oral historian Siobhan McHugh; *Parramatta Girls*, a play by Alana Valentine that traces the legacy of eight Australian women who were institutionalized in a state home for "uncontrollable" girls, and *Run Rabbit Run*, another play by Alana Valentine about an Australian community's struggle to get their rugby team the Rabbitohs reinstated into the National Rugby League. The book also provides a discussion of how verbatim theatre is practiced in Australia, what kinds of stories make good verbatim theatre, and the kinds of issues that arise in creating verbatim theatre.

In Australia, writing and staging a verbatim play usually involves the following practices: a playwright or a team of researchers records an interview with someone, transcribes it, places it alongside other recorded interviews and edits the entire set of interviews into a script that has "dramatic shape." While a verbatim play script is never a word-for-word representation of what has been said in a set of interviews, verbatim playwrights are committed to using the words that appear in the interview transcripts. After a draft script has been written, the artistic team usually conducts a rehearsed reading of the play to provide the interviewees with an opportunity to see how they are going to be represented on stage and give feedback to the team. After a process of consultation and negotiation, the script "stabilizes," and the actors and directors start preparing for public performance.[43]

Turning to a discussion on structuring a verbatim play, Brown provides a helpful set of questions that playwrights might ask themselves about their work: Where is the heart of the project? What is the story you want to tell? What does the research material suggest is the climax of the story? How should the play be sculpted based upon the material? Which characters will be in the play? Are composite characters needed? How will dialogue be constructed out of the monologue interviews that have been collected? What are the particular ethical issues in the project? Will some characters need to be left out? Will some of the interview transcripts need to be edited to create drama?[44]

Building on the questions about ethical issues, Brown provides practical advice for playwrights on how to deal with a variety of ethical issues that arise in verbatim theatre projects, including questions about ownership, interviewing people about sensitive events and the extent to which people whose story is being told should be involved in the editing process. On the question of who owns a story that has been told by a real person to a researcher or theatre artist, Brown suggests consulting all the people involved in a project about who owns what. He then suggests creating a written agreement, contract or release form, which establishes who should be attributed as author and what researchers and artists can and cannot do with the stories they are being told. This is the strategy I used in my *Hong Kong, Canada, Snakes and Ladders* and *Harriet's House* projects. I asked my research participants to sign a consent form that gave me permission to use their words in the form of a play script.

In situations where an interview involves recounting sensitive events, Brown suggests that researchers and artists leave time to debrief after interviews. To remind playwrights what it is like to tell someone a personal story, perhaps a story that has been kept secret until now, he suggests they think about one of their own personal stories and ask themselves the following questions: What would you feel uneasy about a stranger knowing? How would you feel if your story was edited so that only certain parts were used? How would you feel if your story was assigned to a composite character? Would you want your own name attached to the story or would you want to remain anonymous? If you mention other people in your story, do you think you would need their permission?

Finally, on the issue of who should be involved in the editing process and other elements of play creation, Brown suggests a variety of possibilities that could be written up as part of an agreement or release form. For example, research participants could receive the transcript of their interview and be given the opportunity to veto any particular material they don't want used. They can also be given the opportunity to read and comment on an early draft of a script. It is also possible to present a draft script to research participants through preliminary readings and closed performances, as I did with my plays *Hong Kong, Canada* and *Snakes and Ladders*.[45] These preliminary readings provided my research participants with the opportunity to tell me what aspects of the play best represented their stories, what aspects didn't represent their views and perspectives, and what parts of the play they wanted to see revised.

Like Brown, health researcher playwrights Jim Mienczakowski and Teresa Moore are very interested in ethical issues. In an article entitled "Performing Data with Notions of Responsibility" they write that it is important to be mindful of the effect performance texts might have on vulnerable audience members. They offer a set of guiding practices to help health researchers ensure that they "do no harm" when performing their research.[46] These practices include:

- Having healthcare professionals present to counsel members of the audience after the post-performance discussions if required.
- Obtaining ethical clearance from a university ethics committee.
- Engaging in ongoing reflexive and reflective practice during the performance construction process.
- Deliberately choosing data that reveal themes that are positive and hopeful rather than dwelling too much on despair.
- Carefully negotiating with research participants which data are chosen for performance, and ensuring that research participants retain a sense of ownership and authenticity about their lived experiences.
- Ensuring that research participants understand the potential risks that such authenticity brings to performance texts.

Naming research-informed theatre practices

In addition to its in-depth discussion on ethical issues in verbatim theatre projects, the anthology includes a helpful discussion on how to name and categorize different kinds of research-informed theatre projects. Working with the overarching term "reality theatre" (rather than "research-informed theatre") playwright Caroline Wake locates verbatim theatre within a spectrum of six different kinds of theatre practices. Each practice on Wake's continuum highlights the distance between researcher-playwrights and their research-participants.

Reality Theatre					
Autobiographical	Community	Verbatim	Documentary	Tribunal	History[47]

In an autobiographical play, the researcher or original storyteller and the playwright are the same person. Although an autobiographical play may deal with community or social issues, the playwright doesn't necessarily consult with or interview anyone. I saw an example of an autobiographical performance at the 2011 Adelaide Fringe Festival in South Australia. Described as "storytelling" in the Fringe Festival Guide, Andreea Kindryd's performance *From Slavery to Star Trek* took the audience through the history of her family and the history of African-Americans in the United States. She told us about her great-great grandparents and their lives as slaves in Texas. She talked about their son, her great grandfather, who raised seven girls who all became teachers during the Reconstruction period. We heard about her grandmother, who shot two members of the KKK in self-defense and then moved to Watts, California. We listened to the story of how Kindryd's grandfather opened the first Democrat office in California. We heard about her mother's career as a hairdresser, and about the steam burns and "burn burns" that came with straightening Black hair in the 1960s. Kindryd also told stories of her civil rights work with Malcolm X and Martin Luther King: how "Martin" worked on poor people's issues as well as Black people's issues, and how "Malcolm" changed when he went to Mecca. We heard about how Kindryd got a job with the television film company Desilu Productions when Lucille Ball began to hire Black people at the studio. And we heard about her friendship with Ivan Dixon, one of the stars of the television show *Hogan's Heroes*, and the administrative assistant job she was offered on *Star Trek* by writer/producer Gene Coon. Locating a story of her own family history within the history of the United States, Kindryd provided the audience with a personal perspective on the history of racism and race relations in her country.

Community theatre, the second category on the continuum, is made by, with, and about community members. Often, these plays cast community members as themselves in performances of the play. Wake offers two examples of community theatre. In the United Kingdom, a group called Quarantine created a performance called *The Soldier's Song*, which featured serving soldiers as performers. In Australia, the Urban Theatre Project's play *Asylum*, told a set of stories about refugees who had been held in Australian immigration detention centres. In these performances, the performers played themselves and told stories about being soldiers and refugees from their own perspectives.

Verbatim theatre is located in the middle of the continuum, and as discussed earlier, involves having a playwright and/or actors interview members of a community about an issue or event that has affected them. While sometimes community members play themselves, often it is the actors who conducted the interviews who play the interviewees, as in Anna Deavere Smith's *Twilight: Los Angeles 1992*. Sometimes actors who have never met the interviewees play them, as in the V-day productions of Eve Ensler's *The Vagina Monologues*.

Like verbatim theatre, documentary theatre both responds to and represents community issues, but is created through a variety of research materials such as journal entries, media clippings and news footage, in addition to interview material. *The Laramie Project* and *The Pastor Phelps Project* could both be described as documentary theatre although Kaufman uses the term "docudrama" and Newton the term "found text" to describe their work.

As also discussed earlier, tribunal plays are based on official transcripts of judicial proceedings such as a court case or a government inquiry. Unlike verbatim and documentary playwrights, who look for stories that aren't being told elsewhere, tribunal playwrights retell stories that have already been told. As writer Carol Martin explains, tribunal plays "reopen trials in order to critique justice."[48] Although it has also been described as documentary theatre and history theatre, a good example of a tribunal play is Emily Mann's play *The Execution of Justice*.[49]

Finally, writers of history plays, who deal with actual events, consult historical documents. Beverley Cooper and Caryl Churchill worked with historical documents to write *Innocence Lost* and *Top Girls*, and I worked with a variety of historical materials to write *Lost Daughter*, a play about the Toronto Christie Pits Riots in the summer of 1933. Many playwrights consult historical documents but do not include text from these documents in the way that Emily Mann includes text from court transcripts in *The Execution of Justice*. However, some playwrights actually incorporate historical text into their play scripts, like British playwright Rebecca Vaughan. In her biographical play *I, Elizabeth*, Vaughan presents Elizabeth I as a young queen dealing with issues of marriage, succession, religion, war and challenges to her throne.[50] Using only Elizabeth's own letters, speeches and writings, Vaughan explores Elizabeth's struggle to reconcile her own desires for marriage and children with the duties of sovereignty.

Working with Wake's continuum of research-informed theatre practices, *Harriet's House* can best be described as documentary theatre. The play draws upon personal narratives and documentary films written by and about transnational adoptive and same-sex families all over the world, as well as interviews I have undertaken with such families in Toronto.

Summing up

In this first chapter of *Staging Harriet's House* I have engaged in a discussion of research-informed theatre by focusing on American, Australian, British, and Canadian theatre projects that have influenced the development of my own work. I have also located my desire to create performed ethnographies and research-informed theatre within discussions that have taken place within post-modern anthropology and critical teacher education. My work has been a deliberate attempt to engage with the literary turn in American anthropology that began in the mid-1980s. Responding to the argument that ethnographers invent rather than represent ethnographic truths in their ethnographic texts, and inspired by the writing projects described in Ruth Behar and Deborah Gordon's *Women Writing Culture*, I began experimenting with ethnographic playwriting. Twelve years later, my early experiments have evolved into a rigorous program of research-informed theatre. My work as an ethnographic playwright has also been a deliberate attempt to engage my teacher education students in sophisticated reflection on issues of equity and diversity in schooling. I have used several of my research-informed plays in my teacher education classes to provoke important discussions on how to challenge racism and homophobia in classrooms and schools.

In the next chapter, I move on to a discussion of how I wrote and workshopped *Harriet's House*, documenting the process I undertook in collaboration with other theatre artists. The chapter includes a story about why I wanted to write a play about transnational adoption in a same-sex family, the research I undertook as I developed the play, the different kinds of feedback I received as I wrote early drafts of the play, and the four-day workshop that provided me with the opportunity to develop the play with other theatre artists.

· 2 ·

WRITING AND WORKSHOPPING *HARRIET'S HOUSE*

Beginnings

The idea for a playwriting project on transnational adoption emerged in 2006, when I came across an Australian book called *Jesse's World: A Story of Adoption and the Global Family*. Written by journalist Basia Bonkowski, *Jesse's World* tells a set of stories about a transnational adoptive community located in Sydney. An adoptive mother herself, Bonkowski draws from both her own personal experience and from interviews she undertook with nine families in her "global family" to describe what it is like to adopt and be adopted transnationally. The book features the story of one particular child in her adoptive community, Jesse Scott, who is diagnosed with a rare genetic disease of the brain and dies six years after the Scott family adopts him.

My first research-informed theatre project *Hong Kong, Canada* focused on issues of language, loss, culture and race facing Canadian immigrant youth from Hong Kong. I was drawn to Bonkowski's stories of similar issues facing Australian children and youth who had been adopted from countries such as Thailand, Korea and Colombia. Like my play, *Hong Kong, Canada,* which had something important to say to teachers working in multilingual, multicultural classrooms, I thought a research-informed play about mothering across cultural, linguistic and racialized borders would have something important to say about teaching across these borders.

I continued reading other transnational adoption narratives and watching documentary films created by and about adoptive families. Then I began writing a set of ten-minute plays about three different adoptive families. Each play dramatized a particular moment in the lives of the three families. Two of the families had a mother and father who identified as heterosexual. The third family was led by a divorced single mother who had recently come out as a lesbian. Each of the characters in these plays was created from the research I had undertaken. The characters in the ten-minute plays experienced the same conflicts and dilemmas as the families in the personal narratives and documentary films I studied. As I began to write these ten-minute plays, I consulted Gary Garrison's book *Perfect 10: Writing and Producing the 10-Minute Play*, which provided useful writing advice.[1]

I had the opportunity to workshop and perform one of the plays at the 2007 Association of Theatre in Higher Education (ATHE) conference. The conference brings together theatre artists and teachers working in university theatre programs across North America. The association is organized into a variety of focus groups. Each year one of the focus groups, the Playwrights and Creative Teams Focus Group, develops and showcases a number of new scripts through its New Play Development Workshop program. The program is competitive and playwrights who want to participate have to submit an application and a first draft of the script they want to workshop and perform. In a discussion of ten-minute plays, my Spalding mentor Eric Schmiedl once told me that the structure of a ten-minute play requires a playwright to "get in quickly, show conflict, and get out quickly." At the same time, a ten-minute play has to reveal a journey of a character with beginning, middle and end. At the end of the play, the characters have to be different because of the experience they had in the play.

The play I submitted to the ATHE competition was entitled *Seder*, and it told the story of an adoptive mother named Harriet who comes out as a lesbian to her close friend Anita. Although Anita has always invited Harriet's family to her annual Passover Seder, she is reluctant to extend an invitation to Harriet's new girlfriend Marty. Harriet won't go the Seder without Marty, and it is up to David, Anita's oldest adopted son to convince his mother to change her mind. *Seder* was selected for the workshop program, and I was matched up with a dramaturge and director who worked with me for two and a half months to produce a draft of the script that we would rehearse during the conference.

I wrote four drafts of the play before the conference and worked on a fifth draft during the rehearsal period. The play was performed for an ATHE audience on the last day of the conference. My dramaturge was Robyn Quick from Towson University in Baltimore, Maryland, and my director was Barbara Waldinger from Queen's College in Great Neck, New York. I was also provided with a set designer, Charles Erven from Loyola Marymount University in Los Angeles, and three actors: Nancy Lipschultz from Indiana University in Bloomington and Marietta Hedges and Jason Burke from Catholic University in Washington.

I received feedback on the performance from two experienced playwrights: Gary Garrison (the author of *Perfect Ten*) and Paul Lim from the University of Kansas. Gary Garrison's critique focused on three questions: Whose play is it? (Is it Harriet's play or Anita's or David's?) What is the central relationship of the play? (Is it between Harriet and Anita or Anita and David?) What is the play's central conflict? (Is it between Harriet and Anita or Anita and David?) He then asked several other questions: If the central conflict is between the two women, what is at stake for Harriet? If Anita won't accept Harriet's new relationship, what impact will this have on Harriet's life? If the central conflict is between the mother and the son, why is it so important for David that Harriet's girlfriend be accepted? In a similar critique, Paul Kim felt that I was trying to tackle too much in one ten-minute play. There needed to be one central relationship and one central conflict.

The feedback from Garrison and Kim not only helped me re-write *Seder*, it also encouraged me to turn *Seder* into a one-act or full-length play that could hold more than one relationship and more than one conflict. However, with my heavy workload at the University of Toronto, it was difficult to find time to work on a larger project so I continued writing ten-minute plays for another year. Of the three families I had begun dramatizing at the beginning, Harriet's family, was the family that I continued writing about.

The following summer my partner, Margot, and I went to Provincetown, Massachusetts, for a beach holiday. Provincetown is well known in North America as a gay-friendly town. We arrived the week after Provincetown had hosted "Family Week" and there were still lots of same-sex families in town. Many of these families were also mixed-race families. White parents walked up and down Commercial Street with children who were Central-American, Asian, African-American or mixed-raced. Most parents spoke to their children in English, but once, while we were in line waiting for an available bathroom at the public library, a white mother with a Central-American daughter spoke to her little girl in Spanish. Later that night, Jennie McNulty, a white lesbian comedian from Los Angeles made the following joke during her show: "There are a lot of Asians visiting Provincetown this week. They're looking for their children [who have been adopted by the couples vacationing in Provincetown]." The crowd was surprised. A few people laughed quietly, but most were silent, stunned McNulty would go there. One man yelled out, "Oh, nasty." The politics of transnational adoption were embodied in the mixed-race, same-sex families visiting Provincetown, and the tensions brought on by these politics were fuel for the comedians performing there. Before leaving Provincetown I decided to find a way to find the time to research and write a full-length play about Harriet's adoptive family, a play that could explore some of the tensions that I witnessed in Provincetown.

Back in Toronto, I began the 2008 fall semester as the new Chair of my department, a large department with fifty faculty members, eighteen administrative staff and seven hundred and fifty graduate students. I broke down the project of writing *Harriet's House* into six preliminary tasks: (1) continue researching written and filmed narratives about transnational adoptive and same-sex families; (2) interview members of transnational adoptive same-sex families in Toronto; (3) create the characters for the play based on the research; (4) create a story for the play based on the research; (5) create a scene-by-scene outline of the play, and (6) start writing the first draft of the play.

Researching the experiences of transnational adoptive and same-sex families

To find time to continue researching the experiences of adoptive and same-sex families, I hired graduate student Amy Gullage and undergraduate student Dan Parker to participate in a reading group. We met twice a month, discussed a variety of scholarly works on transnational adoption and same-sex families, and linked the issues identified in the work to the personal narratives we were also reading.[2] Amy taught Dan how to write a one-page summary for each article, book chapter or book we were discussing, and we used Dan's summaries to structure our discussions. For each summary, Dan stated the purpose, thesis or main argument of the reading, outlined the key points in point form and concluded with a set of questions he had about the reading and/or the connections he saw between the reading and others we had worked with. If we were discussing an entire book, Dan summarized the introductory and concluding chapter and listed the titles of the other chapters so we could see which, if any, of other chapters we wanted to read together. After several months of reading with Dan and Amy, I began interviewing members of transnational adoptive same-sex families in Toronto. Dan transcribed the interviews.

As briefly mentioned in chapter one, *Harriet's House* was created through a blend of realist, interpretative, and dramatic research and writing techniques. Like other realist ethnographers, I used several methods to collect three types of data: interviews, written narratives and filmed narratives. However, my arguments were not written up as a realist ethnographic text. They were embedded in the fictional storylines in *Harriet's House*.

Realist ethnographers use multiple methods so that they can be more confident of their research findings. By using different methods to get an answer to a research question (for example, What issues do adoptive same-sex families face in their everyday lives?) researchers hope that their mixture of methods will produce similar answers. If too many dissimilar or clashing answers are produced, then researchers know that their research question needs to be reframed or that their methods need to be revised.

Working from an interpretive research paradigm rather than positivist realist paradigm, Laurel Richardson argues that social science researchers shouldn't only be looking for similarities, they should be looking for dissimilarities as well. Working with the concept "crystallization" and the metaphor of a crystal, Richardson challenges the realist idea that research should produce a single, unified truth. Instead, she argues that multiple truths will emerge from a research study.[3] When a research moment or situation is understood to be like a crystal, it can be turned around in many ways to reveal multiple layers of meaning. Just like a crystal can be turned around to reveal multiple layers of light.

In *Harriet's House*, I work with the method of crystallization by presenting multiple perspectives about several issues facing adoptive same-sex families. For example, while one adopted sister in the play, Luisa, continues to speak Spanish in Toronto to stay connected to her birth country, the other sister, Ana, does not. Working with crystallization was key in the *Harriet House* project, as our research revealed that not all adoptees want to return to their birth country or reconnect with their birth culture despite a dominant understanding in the transnational adoption literature that returning "home" to their birth country is vital to adoptees' identity construction and well-being.

Creating characters for *Harriet's House*

One of my favorite ways to begin a new play is by working with a set of exercises I learned from Canadian playwright Kent Stentson at the Prince Edward Island Conservatory playwriting workshop I attended in the summer of 2004. For Kent, the writing of a new play should always begin with character work since it is through the development of characters that playwrights find a story to tell. "Characters," he says, "are the forces which deliver the playwright's messages."

The exercises I learned from Kent involve writing three narratives about a character on my mind. The first narrative is entitled "She" or "He" and is written in the third person. The second narrative is entitled "You" and is written in the second person. The third narrative is entitled "I" and is written in the first person. That fall, I used Kent's exercises to create three characters for *Harriet's House*: Harriet; Luisa, her eldest adopted daughter; and Clare, her youngest birth daughter. I spent half an hour writing each of the narratives and didn't stop writing until the half hour was up. The character work I had already done in my ten-minute plays as well as the research I had undertaken about transnational adoptive families informed the development of these nine early narratives. Here is an excerpt from the third-person narrative I wrote about Harriet. The narrative provided me with some important understandings about Harriet's mothering experiences and her relationship with her adopted daughters Luisa and Ana.

"She"

> She has had a rough time mothering. First, she had to convince her former husband Jonathon to consider adopting a baby from Colombia. Then she had to convince him that they should adopt two children. Two sisters, young girls. No longer babies. No longer even toddlers. Two little girls. Luisa and Ana. Age 10 and age 7 . . . Ana was a delight. Luisa was difficult. Instead of being happy to give up the mothering of Ana to Harriet, Luisa was fiercely protective of her mothering role. Luisa had been Ana's mother for the three years they had spent in the Colombian orphanage. Luisa and Ana's birth mother brought them to the orphanage when Luisa was seven and Ana was four. The birth mother was poor. She was ill. And she couldn't take care of them. Luisa had looked after Ana right from the beginning. She made sure that she had enough to eat, that she was clean, that she wasn't teased by the other kids. She was her mother. For three years. Luisa couldn't give up mothering just because Harriet and Jonathon came along and put them on a plane and took them to North America.

Slowly, Harriet learned to share the mothering with Luisa. She learned to let Luisa dress Ana in the morning even though this was a pleasure that she had anticipated and looked forward to from the day she had seen Ana's picture in the Global Family newsletter that Anita put out. She was allowed to cook for the girls, allowed to clean their rooms, but helping Ana get dressed each morning was Luisa's job. Shopping for clothes was a job that Harriet and Luisa shared. The three of them went to the mall together . . .

By the time Luisa was 11, she was going shopping by herself. Harriet would take both girls down to the mall, start shopping with Ana, letting Luisa go her own way. They would meet for lunch at the food court, then after lunch, Ana and Harriet would take Luisa back to the store that they had shopped at and show Luisa their choices. If there was anything that Luisa really didn't like, they didn't take it . . . Ana liked dressing like a jock. She was very athletic, played girls hockey and liked to wear t-shirts with collars or scooped necks and jeans that fit just right: not too snug and not too big. It wasn't hard to shop for Ana. She usually found what she wanted at the GAP or Old Navy. And her choices were so non-descript that Luisa rarely needed to veto anything. They had learned over the years, Harriet and Ana, how to work with Luisa . . . letting Luisa choose her own clothes wasn't a big deal. She missed the intimate mother-daughter conversations they could have had while shopping, the kinds she sometimes had with Ana once Luisa started shopping on her own. But Luisa didn't seek intimacy from Harriet. They had a very complicated, negotiated relationship. And intimate wasn't the word anyone would use to describe it. Friendly and affectionate at its best, heated and aggressive at its worst. Not exactly the way Harriet had imagined it would be like on the flight to Colombia she and Jonathon took when they went to pick up their new daughters and take them home.

Sometimes when I work with Kent's exercises, a narrative I write for one character ends up providing me with information about another character. In the second-person narrative I wrote about Harriet, I found out more about Luisa. Luisa is the character addressing Harriet as "you" in this next excerpt.

"You"

You try very hard. I know you do. And I'm grateful. I really am. I know I have grown up with privileges that I never would have had if you and Jonathon hadn't adopted us and taken us here. But I don't belong here anymore. It's not your fault. It's not anyone's fault. You did the best you could. I did the best I could. But I don't belong here. And I don't want to belong here. I want to go back home. To Colombia. And as soon as I finish these last few courses, I'm gone. I know you will be disappointed. I know we are going to have a fight. I know you will yell, I know that I will yell, and I know that I will win the argument and that you'll let me go . . . Ana rarely speaks to me in Spanish now. Even when I tell her to speak Spanish with me she won't.

I hate the sound of English coming from her mouth. I feel an ache for the Spanish she used to speak. When I get to Colombia, I won't have to hear Ana speak English. I won't have to hear anyone speak English if I don't want to. You tried. You enrolled us in Spanish classes, though you never took any yourself, we went to Colombia night every year, fundraised for the orphanage. You didn't try to make us forget where we came from. You tried to help us remember. And I remember. And I want to go back . . . You have tried to be a mother. But I never wanted another mother. I had one. She was too sick to take care of us so she sent us to the orphanage. And had she gotten better, she would have taken us back. I was waiting for her to take us back. I wanted to see her but they wouldn't let us. They told us she was too sick. Ana didn't have a mother so I became her mother and we were fine at the orphanage. It was temporary. We were only staying there until our *Mama* got better. I never wanted to be adopted. Other kids did but not me. I wanted to stay in the orphanage, and wait for my mother to get better. They never told us what happened to her. If she got better but moved away, if she didn't get better and died. They said they didn't know. I didn't want to leave until I knew for sure. Knew that she wouldn't come back for us. Ever. I never wanted to go "home" with you. I wanted to wait . . . We've done well enough. You try very hard. But you're not my mother, and I'm not staying here any longer. I'm going home. To my home. To where I come from. To where I belong.

In this last narrative about Harriet, written from the first person, I found out how Harriet feels about coming out as a lesbian in mid-age.

"I"

I have a secret. A secret I've been keeping from everyone, including my daughters. It's not like me to keep secrets. I believe in being as honest and direct as you can. But nevertheless I have a secret. A secret girlfriend. Me. A woman who's been married for 13 years, divorced for three. I'm in love with a woman. A younger woman. Was I always attracted to women and never knew it? Is this something new? A reaction to being divorced? To Jonathon's affair? Does it matter? I'm happy. Really happy . . . The girls. I wonder what they'll think . . . But I have to figure out when. When's the best time. There's probably never a good time to come out to your kids. Come out to your kids. Most people come out to their parents. I'm coming out to my kids. Three teenage daughters. What will they say? And what will my friends say? What will Anita say? Anita will be surprised. Shocked, maybe. But I'm sure she'll be supportive. We've been friends for years now. Eight years. You don't cut someone off after eight years of friendship just because they're gay . . . Surely no one cares if you're gay anymore. I need to tell them. But how? How do you tell your daughters you're gay? How do you answer their questions? If you're so gay, why did you live with Dad for so many years? I don't know. If you don't know, then how do you know you're gay? I just know. How? How do you know? I just know. I can feel it . . .

In Kent's workshop, students took turns reading aloud each of their character narratives and received feedback from Kent and each other. Kent asked us to provide four types of feedback on each of our narratives: a compliment; an image or phrase that stood out; a question that we had about the narrative; and an urge we had in response to what we had heard in the narrative. I really liked Kent's feedback process. When I hear a compliment about my work and hear about an image or phrase that stood out for others before hearing any other feedback, it keeps me open to the questions and urges that follow.

I replicated the feedback process I learned from Kent by asking graduate student Amy Gullage to provide the four types of feedback Kent had asked for. Here is the feedback she gave me for the third-person and the second-person narratives I wrote for Harriet (I hadn't written the "I" narrative in time for our feedback session). In sharing Amy's feedback, it's important to note that Amy had the complete version of narratives, not just the excerpts included above.

After reading the third-person narrative, "She," Amy said she had a good sense of who Harriet was as a person. She wasn't a one-dimensional character. The line in the narrative that stood out for Amy was "This is not how she had imagined it." Amy's question about the narrative was Does Harriet carry any resentment because her life is not what she imagined it would be like? Finally, Amy noted that while Luisa and Ana's birth mother and adoptive father are absent in the story, in their absence they are present. She wanted to see me develop this absence in the story.

After reading the second-person narrative "You" Amy reported that once, again, she had a good sense of who the main character was as a person. While no one line stood or image stood out, Amy did have several questions for me about Luisa:

> What draws Luisa back to Colombia? Is it finding out what happened to her mother? Is it the community she belongs to in Colombia? We know that the girls have been missed. But by whom? When you don't know your history, you have to make it up. What story is Luisa making up?

Amy's urge was to have Luisa know less about her birth mother's life than she does. She believed that this would allow me to create more of a shadow character that could disrupt Luisa's life. Amy's feedback on my early narrative work, particularly her urge to have Luisa know less about her birth mother than she did in the narrative, was very helpful and played a role in how the play continued to develop.

Creating a story for *Harriet's House*

As mentioned earlier, Kent believes that the development of a play's story should emerge from character work. It's interesting to look at the terminology different playwrights use to discuss the process of creating a story for a play script. Following E.M. Forster, Kent distinguishes between the terms "story" and "plot"/"scenario."[4] Forster writes that a story presents "the facts" of a case. It talks about the "who" (the characters), "what" (the narrative push), "where" (the geography or region), and "when" (the time or era). A plot or scenario talks about the "how" and "why" (the motive or motivation of the characters). To illustrate, Forster writes that the sentence "The king died then the queen died" is an example of a story. It states the facts of "who," "what" and "when." However, the sentence "The King died, then the queen died of grief" is an example of plot or scenario. It states "why" the queen died.

In his workshop, Kent had us write a three-page story from our character narratives that only mentioned the facts: who, what, where and when. The story was to be written with a beginning, middle and end. Once again, we read aloud our three-page stories and received feedback in the form of a compliment; an image that seemed important; a quote from the story that resonated with the listener; who the listener thought the main character was and why; a question about the story; and an urge to see something in particular happen in the story. The next assignment was to begin a twenty-five page scenario that added 'how' and 'why' to the story. Following Kent's workshop process, I worked with my nine character narratives and created a story for *Harriet's House*. The final draft of the story follows.

The story of *Harriet's House*

The play begins in the middle of a heated argument between Harriet and her 17-year-old adopted daughter Luisa. Luisa wants to go back to Colombia and work in the orphanage where she spent several years of her childhood but needs Harriet's permission to do so. Harriet, who wants Luisa to attend university in January, refuses to give her permission to go. This is not the first time that Luisa and Harriet have been in a heated argument. They've been arguing from the time that Luisa and her younger sister, Ana, first came to live with Harriet in Toronto. The girls had spent three years together at the orphanage before Harriet and her former husband, Jonathon, adopted them at the ages of seven and ten. It was difficult for Luisa to completely give up mothering Ana, and in the end, both Harriet and Luisa had to learn to share their parenting of Ana. Growing up in Toronto as an adoptee from Colombia hasn't been as easy for Luisa as it has been for Ana. She is determined to go back to Colombia as soon as she can. She has a mission. She wants to find out what happened to her birth mother. Harriet reluctantly gives Luisa permission to return to Colombia to work at the orphanage on the condition that she promises to begin university in the fall.

At the same time as Harriet is getting ready to send Luisa off to Colombia, she is getting ready to come out as a lesbian to Ana and Clare, her third, biological, daughter. Jonathon and Harriet divorced several years ago, and when Harriet began dating again, she discovered she preferred women. She is now in a relationship with a woman named Marty, who wants Harriet to come out; however, Harriet wants to wait until Luisa leaves for Colombia. After Luisa leaves, Harriet comes out to Ana and Clare, and to Anita, a close friend and the founder of the international adoption agency that Harriet and Jonathon worked with when they adopted Luisa and Ana. While Ana and Clare embrace Marty as Harriet's new partner, Anita does not. Harriet knows she has to come out to Luisa as well, but keeps putting it off.

At the end of the summer, Luisa reluctantly returns to Harriet's house to go to university. She hasn't found out any information about her birth mother, and wants to go back to continue her search. Unfortunately, Harriet never did find the right moment to come out to Luisa, and when she does tell her, Luisa is angry that she is the last to know about Marty. Feeling isolated from the family, which has changed while she has been away, Luisa reneges on her promise to go to university and returns to Bogotá.

Several months after Luisa has returned to the orphanage, Harriet is diagnosed with breast cancer. She decides to travel to Bogotá with Marty, Ana and Clare to ask Luisa to come home. When Harriet and her family arrive in Colombia, they find out that Luisa and Ana's birth mother died very soon after she left her daughters at the orphanage. For the last year and a half, Luisa's purpose was to find her mother. Having lost that purpose, she's at a loss of what to do next. Before coming to Bogotá, Clare led a fundraising campaign at her school to raise money for the orphanage, and has come to Colombia with a $10,000 cheque. When Clare proposes beginning a second campaign to raise money for a medical clinic, Harriet suggests Luisa come back to Toronto to raise money and spend some time with the family. She tells Luisa that her sisters need her. After talking with Ana, Luisa decides to return to Toronto.

The play ends with Harriet and Marty deciding to get married to give their same-sex adoptive family social and legal legitimacy, illustrating once again, the complexities of living and loving in a same-sex, adoptive family.

From a story to a scene-by-scene outline of the play

During the first few weeks of fall semester I developed a first draft of the story shared above and created six characters for the play. I decided not to expand the story into a scenario, but to create a scene-by-scene outline of the play instead. I was taught how to create this kind of outline by my Spalding mentor Eric Schmiedl. As the following examples from scenes one, two, and three of *Harriet's House* shows, each outline has four components: setting, action, objective, outcome. These examples come from the final draft of my outline.[5]

Scene 1 (December)

Setting: Harriet's kitchen.
Action: Harriet and Luisa are arguing in the kitchen.
Objective: Luisa wants Harriet to give her permission to go to Colombia so that she can find out what happened to her birth mother.
Outcome: Harriet gives Luisa permission to go to Colombia but only if she promises to come back and do a year of university in Toronto before making a decision about where to live.

Scene 2 (December)

Setting: Harriet's kitchen
Action: Marty is visiting Harriet and her daughters after school.
Objective: Marty wants Harriet to come out to her daughters before Christmas.
Clare wants to learn Spanish, so that she can connect to her sisters by using the language they sometimes use with each other.
Outcome: Harriet won't come out to her daughters before Christmas.
Luisa promises to write to Clare in Spanish.

Scene 3 (March: Three months later)

Setting:	Harriet's kitchen.
Action:	Marty is helping Ana tape up her hockey stick.
Objective:	Ana wants Marty to coach her hockey team. Ana wants to find out if Harriet and Marty are girlfriends.
Outcome:	Marty tells Ana she and Harriet are girlfriends. Marty agrees to become Ana's coach.

After completing the scene-by-scene outline, I began writing a first draft of the play integrating some of the writing from ten-minute plays I had completed. Needing a set of deadlines to keep me writing while I chaired my large department, I enrolled in another on-line playwriting course with the Gotham Writing Workshop. Like the first course I took with Gotham, I had the opportunity to submit scenes from my emerging play to my classmates and instructor Richard Caliban for feedback. By the end of the course and the end of the 2008 fall semester, I had a plan of how I wanted to revise and complete the first draft of the play.

As I worked to complete the first draft of the play in the Spring of 2009, I was still researching transnational adoption and same-sex families with my students Amy Gullage and Dan Parker. Our regularly scheduled meetings provided a space to make sure that the emerging story and script reflected the research findings and what we were reading. By the end of the Spring semester I had a first draft of the script to share with director Jocelyn Wickett. Jocelyn provided feedback on the first draft, and I worked to revise the script in time for a four-day workshop on *Harriet's House* Jocelyn conducted in July.

Revising the play

Each major revision of the script featured two kinds of changes: changes that would improve the drama and theatricality of the script, and changes that would more deeply reflect the research that informed the script. For example, just before the first rehearsal for the Pride Festival production at Hart House Theatre, I started reading a book of essays by Cheri Register called *Beyond Good Intentions: A Mother Reflects on Raising Internationally Adopted Children*.[6] As a mother of two adult daughters whom she adopted as infants from Korea, Register had insights about transnational adoption that were not yet reflected in my script. While I had not intended to make any more changes to draft four of the script before the first rehearsal, Register's insights were too important to leave out. So I revised the script once again.

Register's ten essays focus on ten choices well-meaning adoptive parents make that she feels do not serve adopted children well. The choices Register writes about include wiping away children's pasts, hovering over "troubled" children, holding the lid on sorrow and anger, and believing race doesn't matter. The issue of believing race doesn't matter had appeared in several of the narratives I had read, but had not yet been taken up in the script. I integrated the issue into the conversation that Harriet and Marty have in scene II, about Luisa leaving for Colombia. As mentioned earlier, in Scene II, Marty tells Harriet that she needs to come out to her daughters before Luisa leaves. Harriet answers that adoptive parenting has been more complicated than she thought it would be, and coming out before Luisa's first trip back to Colombia is difficult. What changed in draft five of the script from draft four was the way in which Harriet talked about the difficulties of adoptive parenting.

Excerpt from Scene 2: Draft 4

MARTY: *(Squeezes her hand)* You need to tell them. It's been six months. You've got to trust that they won't reject you. Luisa shouldn't leave for Colombia without knowing.

HARRIET: *(Still holding* MARTY's *hand)* I know, I know. It's just that . . . I had no idea how difficult adolescence was going to be. I never expected Luisa to feel so compelled to find out how her mother died. I always thought we'd go back to Colombia as a family, the four of us, when the girls were a little older. And now she's going back all alone, without—

*(*CLARE, *age 11, calls out from offstage.* HARRIET *drops* MARTY's *hand.)*

Excerpt from Scene 2: Draft 5

MARTY: *(Squeezes her hand)* You need to tell them. It's been six months. You've got to trust that they won't reject you. Luísa shouldn't leave for Colombia without knowing.

HARRIET: I know, I know. It's just that . . . I had no idea how difficult it was going to be. In the beginning, it was all so simple. There were children out there who needed a home. I had a home. There were children who needed a family. I wanted a family. The children were from Colombia. So what? I always thought that when the time came, we'd go back to Colombia together, all four of us. I never imagined that Luisa would insist on going back by herself, that—

*(*CLARE, *age 11, calls out from offstage.* HARRIET *drops* MARTY's *hand.)*

In draft four, Harriet frames the difficulties of adoptive parenting in terms of her naiveté about what adolescence would be like and how her daughters would feel about returning to their birth country. In draft five, she frames the difficulties a little differently, in terms of her naiveté about how her daughters would feel about returning to their birth country, and the importance of race: "The children were from Colombia. So what?"

A revision process that works towards improving the storytelling *and* deepening the presentation of research findings is demanding. I found I needed to be particularly alert to moments where I might be tempted to sensationalize the research findings, or polarize issues in order to create a more dramatic storyline.

Workshopping *Harriet's House*

Harriet's House is the third play that my theatre company Gailey Road Productions has produced for the stage. There are three core members of the company. I am the founder and one of the company's two artistic directors. Jocelyn Wickett is the other artistic director and Gillian Lewis is the production manager. The three of us planned the *Harriet's House* workshop together and took on the roles of playwright (me), director (Jocelyn) and workshop manager (Gillian).

I decided to create my own theatre company after several years of submitting my plays to professional theatre companies and not having any success in getting any of them produced for a public audience. Gailey Road Productions was established in 2007 so I could produce my play *Pound Predators* as part of the Toronto Fringe Festival. The following year, I produced my play *Lost Daughter* at the Fringe. Two years later, *Harriet's House* was produced as part of the Toronto Pride Festival.

The four-day workshop for *Harriet's House* was held in my department's large meeting room, to which I had access as a faculty member in the department. Jocelyn, Gillian and I hired five Toronto actors of different ages to work with us. Two of the actors, Sochi Fried and Jorie Morrow, had worked with Gailey Road Productions before. Jorie had a lead role in our Fringe production of *Pound Predators* and Sochi a lead role in *Lost Daughter*. Gillian set up pre-workshop interviews with the actors we hadn't worked with before, and we hired Clare Acott, Lara Arabian and Sora Olah.

In a planning meeting with Jocelyn and Gillian about the questions that I wanted answered during the workshop, I came up with the following list:

1. What insights do the actors have about each of the characters based on their first reading of the play?
2. What new insights emerge when the actors explore the dialogue and voice of each of the characters?
3. What new scenes might be written to incorporate the insights that emerge in the workshop?

Amy Gullage continued to work with me and joined the workshop team as the workshop ethnographer. A main aspect of Amy's role as ethnographer was to keep a record of how the theatrical work of the workshop related to the research work I had undertaken. As well, at the end of each workshop day she interviewed me about the work that had been accomplished that day. Amy asked me questions about what I liked about the work that had taken place that day, what part of the work I had questions about, what surprised me, and what I might do differently in the next draft of the script. These interviews were audio-taped.

Jocelyn began the four-day workshop with a reading of the entire script, which was in its second draft. The reading was immediately followed by a discussion of why I had written the play, and then by a discussion of the actors' first impressions. Next, Jocelyn led the group in a separate reading and discussion of each scene. After this work, the actors put the scene "on its feet" by standing up and moving around. This second reading was followed by another discussion. Sometimes the second scene discussion led to improvisation work. Sometimes it led to an improvisation of a possible new scene. Gillian audio-taped some of the discussions and videotaped some of the improvisations so that I would have a record of the work undertaken during the workshop.[7] I rewrote the script based on what I learned about the characters and the story from the workshop, keeping the research I had undertaken at the centre of revision decisions.

Locating myself in *Harriet's House*

Jocelyn's request for me to talk about why I had written *Harriet's House* on the first day of the workshop was for me to personally locate myself in the project. It is a request I often receive from people who have read the play, or seen it performed. People want to know if my partner Margot and

I have adopted children ourselves and if I am writing from the position of an adoptive mother. While Margot and I do not have any children of our own, we are a same-sex family. Like Harriet and Marty, we find ourselves discussing if, when and how to come out as a same-sex family to people who do not know that we are a couple. Like Harriet and Marty, we recently got married to give our long-term relationship social legitimacy. These life experiences have had an influence on why and how I have written *Harriet's House.*

My desire to write about adoption in a same-sex family from outside the position of an adoptive mother, however, has to do with the lack of representation of such families in the educational literature I have read, and in popular culture, more generally. In the early and mid-1990s, very few of our friends and colleagues in same-sex families were raising children. Two decades later, many more are. Yet, there are still very few stories about this new generation of same-sex families, whether they are adoptive or non-adoptive.

When I began writing my 10-minute plays in 2005, one of the issues I had to work through was how to create a transnational adoptive same-sex family. At the time, two same-sex partners could not (and still cannot) be "out" as a couple and adopt transnationally.[8] One partner can try to adopt as a single parent, but has to hide or lie about his or her same-sex family life. As I was thinking about how to create Harriet's family[9] I came across the work of Josefina López, an American playwright who wrote *Real Women Have Curves.*[10] On her website, López posted some advice for writers. One piece of advice was this:

> Take all your disadvantages and flaws and make them into assets by asking yourself: In what world is it okay to be me? Create that world. With your vision you give other people the inspiration to create a world where they too belong.[11]

Harriet's House presents a world in which it is okay to be out as a transnational adoptive same-sex family. And this is important, because living in a family like Harriet's can be complicated and challenging. As Toby Alice Volkman writes, living in a transnational adoptive family provokes a number of questions about race, culture, and nation; Questions about genes, kinship, and belonging; Questions about the politics of sending and receiving nations.[12] Living in a same-sex family provokes additional questions about homophobia, social legitimacy, and legal rights for same-sex families. *Harriet's House* takes up many of these questions. The play also provides adoptive same-sex families with an opportunity to see themselves represented on stage and consider how one family works through the complexities and challenges of everyday life.

This is why I have written the play. As well, as discussed in Chapter One, when *Harriet's House* is read aloud in my teacher education classes, opportunities open up for teachers to question the beliefs and attitudes they hold about families that are different from their own. This, too, is why I have written the play.

Important moments in the workshop

The four-day workshop Jocelyn designed and facilitated provided a space for the actors to embody the six characters portrayed in *Harriet's House* and to explore their relationships with one another. As the creator of the play, I worked closely with the workshop team, sharing what I knew about each of the characters and their connections to each other. Jocelyn remembers the team learning a lot from my talking about why I wrote the play. I remember gaining both clarifying and new insights about the play by watching the team bring the characters to life. What follows is a discussion of several important moments in the workshop that influenced the way I revised the script.

Discussing the play's storyline and structure

As mentioned earlier, after the first read-through, the actors provided me with their first impressions of the play. Their questions about the timeline of different events in the story helped me understand what parts of the story were not yet clear, and how revised scenes or new scenes might fill in the holes of the story. For example, during the first read-through, it was not clear to the actors how long Harriet and Marty had been together. There were also questions about the extent to which Marty might want to become involved with the care of Harriet's daughters. These were questions I kept in mind as I continued to develop the play.

Another important discussion that took place on the first day had to do with the structure of the play. In the workshop draft of the script, I had located my scenes in a variety of settings. Jocelyn believed that given the budget and design limitations we faced, our Pride production of *Harriet's House* would work best if the story could be contained within two or three settings. She suggested that I begin the story in Harriet's kitchen, move it to Colombia, and then move it back to the kitchen. My challenge in revising the workshop script was to keep the story going in only two spaces: the kitchen, and a bench outside the orphanage in Colombia.

One of the joys of hearing actors read *Harriet's House* aloud for the first time was finding out that the play had emotional power. I could feel that power in the pit of my stomach as the actors read through the scene where Anita refuses to accept Harriet's new relationship and refuses to invite Marty to Seder. The actors also commented on how emotionally charged the play was, and in our interview at the end of the first day of the workshop, Amy commented that the play "tapped a nerve." Knowing that the play had emotional power provided me with a clear indication that it was a piece I should keep working on.

Deepening the characters

While the first day's work focused on the play's storyline and structure, the second day focused on character development. Each of the actors used their own personal experiences to find a personal entry point into the play and talk about its characters. For example, one actor used her own experience as an adopted child to talk about Luisa and Ana's experiences. Another talked about growing up biracial. She shared her own understandings of the cultural and racial issues Luisa and Ana face as young women who were born in Colombia but are growing up in Canada. A third actor found her way into the story by connecting to Harriet's mothering.

Moving in and out of collaboration

As the day unfolded, some of the actors became heavily invested in how individual characters might be developed. In my interview with Amy at the end of the day, I commented that this investment was a wonderful thing because it meant that my characters' experiences were resonating with the actors, to a point where they were fighting for a particular representation of a character in the script. However, I also commented that this was difficult thing because there were now multiple investments circulating in the workshop and I was really not sure what to do with them all. I needed to filter which of the reponses made sense to the development of the play, and which did not.

I decided to make five copies of the play, one for each day of the workshop and a fifth copy to integrate all of the feedback that made sense. On copies one, two, three and four I took notes on all the feedback I received during each of the four days of the workshop. As a set, the four scripts provided me with a rich set of possible pathways for developing the play. I began working on a revision plan (which was eventually outlined on the fifth copy of the script) by returning to the goal of the play, what I wanted the story to do.

In reviewing the feedback documented on the four workshop scripts, I asked myself: What might push the story I want to tell forward? While I worked with all the contributions that were made in the workshop, in the end I didn't give voice to every contribution in the revised script. Like Caryl Churchill, who often engages in workshops of her plays, I began rewriting after the workshop, and maintained ultimate responsibility for the rewriting of the script.[13]

Amy understood this strategy as "moving in and out of collaboration" and commented that it resonated with research approaches undertaken in feminist research. For Jocelyn, the team's collaborative work throughout the entire project could be seen as an example of feminist theatre practice. In an e-mail message about my participation in both the workshop and the rehearsal process Jocelyn wrote:

> By being involved in the workshop and rehearsal process you were able to support the evolution of the script and work out the kinks by seeing your creation in front of you. This sets you apart from other playwrights who believe their work is done when they finish their "perfect script" and hand it over as a stable piece that is completed. Whether it was about character or plot or how Harriet would keep her kitchen, you were part of the process and the creative integrity that made *Harriet's House* what it is. The whole team was. We carved out a set of feminist theatre practices and the way we worked together, created together, had an impact on the integrity of this piece of research-informed theatre. Our work was never done, always changing, shifting, evolving, as life does and perspective does, as truth does.[14]

Elaborating on my description of moving in and out of collaboration during the workshop, Jocelyn wrote that our collaborative practice took different forms during different moments of the production process.

> You were solely responsible for the development of the script and ultimately responsible for the text as it developed. You moved in and out of collaboration with the rest of us then. During the rehearsal process I think that you and I moved in and out of collaboration. As well, the actors and myself moved in and out of collaboration. Sometimes [during the rehearsal process] an actor would offer something and would really want to try it. We would explore it in rehearsal, but if it didn't work, I wouldn't use it. Additionally, [during the rehearsal process] you and I talked about the script . . . Some things were up for interpretation and some things you already knew what you wanted and it was up to me to translate your vision to the actors.
>
> I also think that the process of directing *Harriet's House* and that relationship between the research, the script and rehearsals is very different from the relationship

between the script and a reading in a teacher education class. The script is used differently and the impact or experience of the play as a reader is different from the impact and experience as an audience member.[15]

Learning from scene work

The goal of the scene work undertaken on days two, three and four of the workshop was to provide me with an opportunity to hear how each scene sounded when read aloud. The team's scene-reading discussions focused on lines that did not work well, lines that the actors did not think their characters would say, lines that were repetitive, and lines that were too obvious. These discussions helped me improve a number of individual scenes in the script. The team also looked at places in a scene where I was telling the audience something rather than showing it to them. Showing, not telling, is much more theatrical.

When the actors put a scene on its feet, I learned how different movements worked with particular lines to produce different emotional moments on stage. This helped me to think about what kinds of stage directions needed to be put into the script so that a similar emotion could be evoked during a future performance of the play. As mentioned earlier, sometimes Jocelyn asked actors to improvise on a scene that was on its feet, to provide me with more information about a character or about Harriet's family. For example, she asked two actors to improvise Luisa and Ana coming home from school before starting Scene II, so that I could hear what everyday family life in Harriet's house sounded like. Some of the lines that were created in this improvisation appear in the current draft of the script.

On the afternoon of the fourth day of the workshop, the actors improvised scenes that I thought I needed to add to the script. One of these scenes, the scene where Marty moves into Harriet's house, appears in the current script. These improvised scenes represent the workshop's most engaged collaborative moments. The work that was undertaken was no longer just mine. The team created new dialogue based on what they already knew about the characters and the story. Over the four days, then, the collaborative process of the workshop deepened. The team moved from reading the play together for the first time and finding common ground by working with a common text, to discussing each scene in the text, to deepening the discussion of the text by putting scenes on their feet, to creating new text together through improvisation.

In our last interview together, Amy asked me if I would undertake a similar workshop again. I responded, "In a heartbeat." I felt that a new bar had been set for me around creating new work. I knew that the collaborative work undertaken in the workshop would enable me to produce a far superior piece of work to what I would have been able to produce on my own. The workshop had been a gift.

Budgeting for the workshop

Like a production of a play, a workshop needs to be budgeted for. I kept my budget plan simple, listing the expenses into four categories: honoraria for the artistic team, fees, meals, and supplies.

One of the actors on the team was a member of the Canadian Actors' Equity Association (CAEA), an organization that represents professional artists working in theatre, opera and dance in English Canada (Union des Artistes [UdA] represents actors in Quebec and other French-language theatres). This meant I needed to contact CAEA to make sure that the workshop honorarium I was paying the actors was in line with the CAEA guidelines. It also meant that I had to pay CAEA a fee for their assistance in helping me hire a CAEA actor. The four-day workshop cost about $2,300 to run. This amount did not include Amy's time, which was funded by the Ontario Institute for Studies in Education (OISE)'s Graduate Assistant (GA) program, which provides full-time graduate students with an opportunity to develop their research skills by working on professors' research projects.

The 2009 International Women's Playwright Conference

The next step of script development involved presenting a reading of scenes from the third draft of *Harriet's House* at the 2009 International Women's Playwright Conference in Mumbai, India. The conference, which takes place every three years, has brought women playwrights, theatre artists, cultural workers and scholars together since 1986. The reading in Mumbai gave me the opportunity to solicit feedback from women playwrights working in Norway (Kristin Bjorn), India (Hina Siddiqui), New Zealand (Denise Walsh), Australia (Fiona Wheeler), the United States (Vanessa Adams-Harris), as well as Canada (Beverly Cooper, Marcia Johnson, Gaily Nyoka, Sally

Stubbs, and my partner, Margot Huycke, who travelled to the conference with me). Inspired by what I learned about my characters and my story from the feedback I got from the conference reading, I began another set of revisions of the play and completed a fourth draft of the script.

Finally, in preparation for two grant applications to help fund the production of *Harriet's House* due in February 2010, several months before the beginning of rehearsals, I solicited feedback on the post-conference draft from Toronto editor and poet Sharon Singer, who was the facilitator of my writing group The Moving Pen. I had joined the group in the fall of 2009, the second year of my two-year term as department chair, to make sure that I would spend at least several hours a week engaging in creative writing. My writing group met once a week and provided two and a half hours of "writing practice" each week through a set of different writing prompts. The first prompt was a picture cut out of a magazine. The rest of the prompts were quotes from writings by other writers. Sharon provided us a particular amount of time to write on each prompt. We could write whatever we liked as long as we kept the pen moving and didn't stop writing. In addition to running her Moving Pen workshops, Sharon also works as a writing mentor and editor. Before sending a sample of the script along with my Ontario and Toronto Arts Council grant applications, I asked her to read the latest draft of *Harriet's House*. One of the substantial issues that Sharon raised was the fact that play had the family working through a lot of issues all at the same time. She suggested that I eliminate two of the issues that had been mentioned in the play but that hadn't been developed. Sharon's feedback was key to tightening up the script for the arts council grant proposals I wrote to fund the production in February 2010.

One of the joys of writing plays is collaborating with others to create a well-written script. Over the four years I developed *Harriet's House*, I worked with many other playwrights, writers and theatre artists to create the strongest script I could. However, while *Harriet's House* was able to incorporate many of the issues that emerged from my research with some nuance and depth, at the end of play, there was still much more to say.

New beginnings

After the show had been staged at Hart House Theatre, a number of audience members wanted to know what happens to Harriet and her family. I continued reading about transnational adoption, this time focusing on the perspectives from an emerging field called the "new adoption studies," which features research and writing done by adult adoptees.[16] Reading in this area deepened my understandings of the issues that were taken up in *Harriet's House* and I decided to write a sequel to the play that would feature a story of Harriet's younger adopted daughter Ana. The play, which is now in its fourth draft, has the working title of *Ana's Shadow*, and has allowed me to deepen the experiences of adoptive and same-sex family life that were presented in *Harriet's House*. Once again, I have begun the cycle of researching, writing, workshopping and revising.

Deepening my story of Harriet's family

Recent research and writing from the new adoption studies understands transnational/transracial adoption as "the intimate face" of colonization, racism, militarism, imperialism, and globalization.[17] The literature describes adoptees' experiences of racism, isolation, abuse, depression, addiction and alienation, and in doing so, indicates that transnational/transracial adoption can result in emotional and spiritual costs for adoptees. It also directs attention to the need for long-term solutions that address the root causes leading to children of color being removed from their families or surrendered for adoption. However, writing from the new adoption studies also demonstrates the ways transnational/transracial adoptees have been able negotiate a variety of tensions within their adoptive families, rebuild connections to communities and families of origin, make productive meaning of their adoption and create new identities based on their life experiences. My reading in the new adoption studies has provided me with additional research material to begin a play that continues the story about all the members of Harriet's family but that focuses on Ana.

Ana's Shadow begins three years after *Harriet's House* ended. In the current fourth draft of the play (which will change as the play continues to develop), Harriet is undergoing cancer treatment for the second time and 19-year-old Ana's reaction is pure panic. To her family's dismay, she drops out of university and spends her days taking Harriet to chemotherapy, helping her keep the household going, and when she has time, writing songs. Ana's journey in the play is to learn to live beside her fear of losing Harriet to cancer and to find the confidence to perform as a singer songwriter.

While Ana takes over the shopping, cooking and cleaning on the days Harriet is feeling sick from chemo, 22-year-old Luisa is planning a return trip to Bogotá with 16-year-old Clare. They are going to begin building a health clinic next to the orphanage Luisa and Ana lived in as children, a project the family has spent the last three years fundraising for. While she is in Bogotá, Luisa hopes to find members of her birth family.

Unlike Luisa, Ana has no interest in going to back to Bogotá or reconnecting with her birth family. As mentioned earlier, our research revealed that not all adoptees want to return to their birth country despite a dominant understanding in the transnational adoption literature that returning "home" to their birth country is key to adoptees' well-being.[18] Similarly, not all adoptees want to reconnect with their birth family. In *Harriet's House*, this perspective was not developed. The play focused on Luisa's journey back to Colombia to find her birth mother and her excitement about returning to her birth country. In *Ana's Shadow*, Ana provides a different perspective on returning "home." In the scene that follows, Luisa is now in Bogotá and Anita asks Ana if she's heard from her. Ana and Luisa had a falling out before Luisa left and Ana hasn't been in contact with her. Marty is also in this scene.

Excerpt from scene 10 in *Ana's Shadow* (draft 4, August 2011)

ANITA: *(To ANA)* Have you heard from Luisa?
ANA: Clare has.
ANITA: And?
ANA: They've finished the foundation of the clinic.
ANITA: That's exciting!
(ANA shrugs.)
Has she started looking for your family?
(ANA shrugs.)
You don't know?
ANA: No.
ANITA: You don't want to know?
ANA: No.
ANITA: I see.
ANA: Do you think that makes me weird?
MARTY: *(Definite)* No. That doesn't make you weird.
ANA: Everybody thinks I should be interested in going back to Colombia to find my birth family. Or that I should be interested in building the clinic. Like Luisa. But I'm not. It's her thing. Not mine.
MARTY: And that's fine. There are other ways you can support the clinic. You don't have to go there and build it.
ANA: And they think that when you go back to your birth country, you automatically fall in love with it because it's the place where you really belong.
(MARTY is quiet.)

ANITA: *(Also quiet, then)* But that doesn't always happen.
ANA: No! When we went back to bring Luisa home I didn't fall in love with Bogotá. I didn't even like it. It was hot. It was noisy. It was poor. I didn't feel like I belonged there. I didn't feel like it was my real home. And when we went to visit the orphanage I started imagining what would have happened to us if Harriet hadn't adopted us. It was terrifying. You know?

Ana's admission that she didn't like Bogotá when the family went to visit Luisa at the end of *Harriet's House* challenges the idea that all adoptees inevitably wish to return to where they "really" belong. In a later scene in the play, Ana speaks to Clare about her lack of interest in meeting her birth family. In the scene Clare, who unlike Ana, speaks to Luisa regularly, knows that Luisa has found their deceased birth mother's sister.

Excerpt from scene 14 in *Ana's Shadow* (draft 4, August 2011)

CLARE: *(Very careful)* So if I had some news about Luisa finding someone from your birth family, would you want to know about it?
ANA: She found someone?
(CLARE nods.)
Who?
CLARE: Your mother's sister. Your aunt.
ANA: Really?
CLARE: Yeah.
ANA: Well, I'm happy for her. For Luisa, I mean, because it means something to her. But it doesn't mean anything to me.

The differences in the ways Ana and Luisa feel about their birth country and their birth family are meant to underscore an important idea that Cheri Register shares in her book of essays on transnational adoption: Adoptees are the only ones who can make personally useful sense of their adoption.[19] While Luisa goes back to the orphanage to build a health clinic, Ana begins to write songs about her years in the Colombian orphanage she was adopted form.

Over the three years that she has worked with her family to raise money to build the clinic, Luisa has developed a more sophisticated understanding of the politics of transnational adoption. In *Ana's Shadow*, she raises questions about transnational adoption that allow me to deepen the work of *Harriet's House* in another way. The following discussion between Luisa and Anita (before she leaves to Bogotá) is informed by my reading in the new adoption studies. Harriet's insight about the joy and the injustice of transnational adopting living side-by-side is informed by Cheri Register's introductory essay in *Beyond Good Intentions*.

Excerpt from scene 6 in *Ana's Shadow* (draft 4, August 2011)

ANITA: *(Indignant)* So now you're saying I'm an unethical person.

LUISA: I didn't say that.

ANITA: Yes, you did.

LUISA: No, I didn't. I said that transnational adoption is a way of supplying wanna-be parents in rich countries with children from poor countries. And I—

ANITA: I'm unethical because I find homes for orphaned children.

LUISA: When poor parents have to send their children to an orphanage because they can't take care of them, and then parents from rich countries go to those countries to adopt those children because they *can* afford to take care of them, then that's—

ANITA: Every child deserves a home.

LUISA: Every mother deserves to bring up her own children.

ANITA: It's better for children to live in an orphanage than live with a family?

LUISA: No. But it's not only a matter of child welfare, it's also a matter of—

ANITA: Yes or no? Living in a family is better than living in an orphanage.

LUISA: It's not only about—

ANITA: Yes or no? Your life here with Harriet is better than it would have been if you had stayed in the orphanage?

LUISA: Yes.

ANITA: Yes or no? Adoption saves children from homelessness.

LUISA: Some children, yes, but—

ANITA: Yes or no? Adoption saves children from disability, from dying?

LUISA: Yes. But why do children from poor families need to be adopted to get medical care?

ANITA: I can't answer that question. Life's unfair. And I refuse to be blamed for all the injustices of the world.

LUISA: I'm not blaming you. This isn't about you. It's about resisting the idea that transnational adoption is a panacea—

ANITA: Overseas adoption is a fine way to form a family.

LUISA: But it comes with problems.

ANITA: All families have problems.

LUISA: Particular kinds of problems. Being separated from your biological family. Being displaced to a culture that's not your own. Growing up in a family that's white when you're not.

ANITA: You seem to be doing just fine.

LUISA: *(To Harriet with affection)* I've been lucky.

ANITA: So maybe I'm not so unethical after all. I matched you up with Harriet.

LUISA: *(To Harriet)* Help me!

ANITA: You don't agree with her?!

HARRIET: I understand her argument.

ANITA: What argument? That you're unethical because you adopted her and Ana? Because you took them away from their cultural roots?

HARRIET: No. That what was supposed to be a temporary welfare measure has become an ongoing source of revenue in some countries. That sometimes adoption is a safety valve that delays social reform.

ANITA: So you regret adopting them?

HARRIET: No! Of course, not. I can believe what Luisa says is true and at the same time not regret adopting them.

ANITA: And how does that work?

HARRIET: When I look at things up close, right in front of me, I have my own personal joy of living with Luisa and Ana. But when I move back, I can see the injustice of parents having to give up their children to keep them alive and healthy. The joy and the injustice live side-by-side.

ANITA: The injustice is that there are still too many children waiting for families. And that's something I can do something about.

LUISA: And that there are still too many mothers dying of illnesses that they don't need to die from. That's something *I* can do something about.

Writing a sequel to *Harriet's House* to reflect multiple perspectives about transnational adoption reminds me once again of Yvonne Lincoln's suggestion that if all texts are only partial and historically- and culturally-situated, there is only a limited chance that the multiple understandings that come from a research project can be presented in a single text.[20] In *Ana's Shadow* Luisa, Ana and Clare grow up and Harriet and Marty's relationship deepens and matures. Marty's relationship to Harriet's three daughters also deepens and matures. The play provides an opportunity to build on the issues raised in *Harriet's House* and to present a wider variety of experiences of living in an adoptive same-sex family living beside cancer.

Summing up

The story of how I wrote and workshopped *Harriet's House* is a story of collaboration with other playwrights and theatre artists. I have been fortunate to have been able to participate in a number of playwriting development initiatives such as the Prince Edward Island Conservatory playwriting workshop and the Association of Theatre in Higher Education's new play development program. I have also been fortunate in finding a group of thoughtful and talented theatre artists in Toronto who brought the characters in *Harriet's House* to life. In the next chapter I move on to a discussion of assessing research-informed theatre. Working with a set of five criteria put forward by American sociologist Laurel Richardson, I engage with questions of social contribution, aesthetic merit, accountability, and ethical practice.

· 3 ·

ASSESSING RESEARCH-INFORMED THEATRE AND *HARRIET'S HOUSE*

As an interdisciplinary activity that is practiced in both the academic and the theatre worlds, there are a variety of reasons why research-informed theatre needs to be assessed. In the academy, all research studies need to be evaluated (usually by a process of peer-review) before research findings are deemed credible enough to be published and disseminated. In the theatre, artistic directors and dramaturges read and evaluate scripts every season in the search for new plays to stage at their theatres. Play scripts are also assessed by funding bodies to determine if they merit financial support. Finally, plays are evaluated by theatre critics who make judgments on whether or not they are worthy of an audience's time and attention. Although they get assessed all the time, research-informed theatre scripts can be difficult to evaluate. They are hybrid texts, created by practices that have evolved in two different worlds, each with multiple ways of evaluating the strengths and limitations of individual projects.

American sociologist and autoethnographer Laurel Richardson has developed five criteria for evaluating research projects that make use of "creative analytic practices" in the way that research-informed theatre does.[1] Richardson uses these five criteria when reviewing papers or monographs for social scientific publication, and I use them here as a framework to discuss how research-informed theatre might be assessed. I also use each of Richardson's five criteria to assess the strengths and limitations of *Harriet's House*, illustrating how the framework might be used by other playwrights and researchers to assess both their own and other people's projects

There are several other American sociologists and autoethnographers who have written about assessing creative analytical work. They include Arthur Bochner, Carolyn Ellis, and Norman Denzin, and I include several of their ideas to layer and enrich Richardson's framework in this chapter. While the assessment criteria put forward by Bochner, Ellis and Denzin are particularly useful for evaluating and reflecting upon autoethographic projects, overall I find Richardson's framework is better-suited for assessing my playwriting projects. Richardson's five criteria are substantive contribution, aesthetic merit, reflexivity, impact and ability to evoke lived experience.

Substantive contribution

Richardson's first criterion, "substantive contribution," asks if a project contributes to society's understanding of social life. It also asks if the work is grounded in a social scientific perspective, and how this perspective has informed the writing of the play. This criterion is also important to Carolyn Ellis and Norman Denzin. Ellis writes that she expects a story to tell her something new about social life, the experience of others, the author's experience, and/or the reader or audience's own life.[2] Denzin values projects that present "political, functional, collective and committed viewpoints."[3]

Richardson, Ellis and Denzin's framing of substantive contribution resonates in the theatre world in a number of ways. I see a particularly strong resonance between Richardson's ideas of substantive contribution and the goals of political theatre. While all plays can be considered political, in the sense that they attempt to present a particular point of view as persuasively as they can, theatre writer Hilary Glow defines political plays as those that interrogate systems of power. In her book *Power Plays: Australian Theatre and the Public Agenda*, Glow discusses the work of eight playwrights whose plays attempt to understand how politics shape who people are and how people live and work.[4]

To illustrate, the production of Hannie Rayson's play *Life After George* in 2000[5] by the Melbourne Theatre Company provoked Australian public debate about the impact of economic rationalism on universities. Rayson tells Glow,

> . . . I think because economic rationalism occurs insidiously, people find it hard to pinpoint, and you don't know who is to blame. And every institution, not just the universities, were going through this experience, so naming those things, to say this is actually happening, is very important . . . *Life After George* gave ammunition to people who felt unsettled and yet were too busy at work to figure this stuff out, and it showed that they are part of a growing group of disenchanted folks whose shared values, consensual values, and their belief in core values have been completely undermined.[6]

Similarly, playwright Ben Ellis, who writes about the economic and political downturn of rural communities in Australia, tells Glow that he sees theatre as a "public facilitator":

> Our avenues for political discourse have closed down so much that when we have plays about . . . topics that we haven't really discussed a lot, I think audiences want to hear that . . .[7]

Ellis' play *Falling Petals*, which premiered at the Playbox Theatre in Melbourne in 2003, focuses on youth's experiences in rural Australia. Described as a dark "sci-fi satire" by theatre critics, it is set in the fictional town of Hollow, which has a declining population of just over 10,000 people. Glow writes that most of the action in the play takes place around a cherry blossom tree, which is gradually losing its blossoms. Three friends, Tania, Sally and Phil, are in their final year of high school and are hoping that they will get good enough grades to get into university in the city. They are desperate to escape Hollow, a town that Phil describes as "small and nasty and fucked." Mr. Syme, their careers guidance teacher, however, doesn't believe in giving his students false hope, and discourages them from setting their sights too high. But it is not only the lack of opportunities in Hollow that Phil and his friends want to run away from. The young children in the town are dying of a mysterious illness, which builds into an epidemic in the play. The illness only affects children, starting with the very young and then gradually killing off older school children, until the teenagers themselves are afflicted with "child ridding disease."[8] Glow writes that the play is "savage" in its critique of an older generation, which has disenfranchised and marginalized its young.

Both Rayson's and Ellis' uses of theatre to provoke public discussion and deliberation on current economic and social issues are strong examples of how political theatre, like the research-informed theatre and reality theatre discussed in Chapters One and Two, can contribute to society's understanding of social life.

The contribution of *Harriet's House*

Harriet's House attempts to make a contribution to our understanding of social life by examining the ways that members of a transnational adoptive same-sex family understand and respond to a variety of issues that emerge in their everyday lives. I selected this research topic because of its potential to provoke rich discussions about a wide variety of issues facing diverse Canadian families: issues of social acceptance, race and racism, language use, linguistic and cultural identity, sexual orientation and homophobia. In future teaching with *Harriet's House*, I plan to examine and write about how my teachers engage with the play, and the extent to which their engagement prompts reflection, and perhaps, a questioning of their own beliefs and attitudes about families that are different from their own.

As discussed in Chapter One, *Harriet's House* is informed by the postmodern perspectives that accompanied the literary turn in American anthropology in the mid-1980s. It is also grounded in the perspectives of the current critical teacher education movement in Canada, the United States, Britain and Australia. This movement is concerned with preparing teachers to facilitate academic and social success for all students, across cultural, linguistic and racialized differences. Over the past twelve years, I have been using my ethnographic scripts *Hong Kong, Canada* and *Snakes and Ladders* to support and enrich the work I do to prepare teachers for working in diverse classrooms across Canada and internationally. In the last decade, these performed ethnographies have been used in teacher education classrooms and conferences in Australia (Brisbane, Sydney, and Toowoomba), Brazil (Sáo Paulo), Singapore and the United States, as well as Canada. Often, issues of diversity and equity are discussed in a depersonalized, distanced manner in teacher education classes. Engaging in the reading of a play script is a powerful way of creating a personal and emotional connection with issues faced by the characters of the play. As discussed in Chapter One, my research on working with research-informed theatre has demonstrated that this kind of connection prompts teachers to reflect upon their understandings and attitudes around multilingualism in the classroom,[9] and supporting lesbian, gay, bisexual, transgender, queer (lgbtq) students at school.[10] I anticipate that *Harriet's House* will be able to do similar pedagogical work around issues of transnational adoption and everyday life in mixed-race, same-sex families.

As discussed in Chapter Two, *Harriet's House* been informed by scholarly writing and narratives (both filmed and written) by and about adoptive families.

Perspectives from the new adoption studies have been particularly helpful in revealing how adoptees negotiate a variety of tensions within their adoptive families, rebuild connections to communities and families of origin, make productive meaning of their adoption, and create new identities based on their life experiences. Luisa's journey in *Harriet's House* is an example this kind of negotiation, rebuilding, and meaning-making.

Finally, Jocelyn Wickett, the director of *Harriet's House*, believes that the play asks the audience to reflect and think about their relationships as lovers, mothers, sisters, daughters, friends. In an artistic statement she prepared for a grant application, Jocelyn wrote:

> *Harriet's House* is a story that is going to bring together an audience of adoptive and same-sex families and provide them with an opportunity to see themselves represented on stage. *Harriet's House* is also a story that is going to enlighten, challenge, inspire and ask us all to reflect upon our own families, relationships, and identities. In telling the stories of six women, their love for one another and their journey together as a family, I want to question and reflect upon the complexities of identity, best intentions, the roles of mother, daughter, sister, and partner, and what it means to be different. Every woman is either or both mother or daughter to someone, and the negotiation, struggle and love for this relationship is at the heart of *Harriet's House*.[11]

Aesthetic merit

Richardson's second criterion asks whether a project has aesthetic merit. Does the project succeed aesthetically? Is the project artistically shaped, satisfying, and complex? Does the playwright's use of dramatic techniques invite interpretive response?[12]

Carolyn Ellis also values aesthetic merit. In a discussion of the importance of "literary value" in creative analytic practice, she writes that she wants to read works that are engaging and nuanced, texts that allow her to feel and think with them. Ellis values "evocation" and wants stories that take her into other worlds, and stories that stay with her after she has read them.[13] Similarly, Arthur Bochner values stories that move his "heart and belly as well as [his] head."[14]

The question of aesthetic merit is related to the form, as well as the content of an individual project. For example, Ben Ellis' science-fiction satire *Falling Petals* and Hennie Rayson's naturalistic or realist play *Life After George* are aesthetically successful in different ways. Ellis' play makes effective use of the techniques of satire while Rayson's story resonates with her audiences' own experiences of economic rationalism.

What makes a play aesthetically successful can be a highly individual call. For example, Glow writes that *Falling Petals* received a mixed critical reception. The theatre reviewer for the *Australian* described the play as clever for exposing the challenges facing rural youth, and praised Ellis' interest in exploring generational divisions without sentimentalizing either side: "In Ellis' view teenagers are truculent animals . . . [and] adults are patronizing tyrants." In this way, the play manages to be "tough, unsettling theatre that reaches for the jugular."[15] The reviewer for the *Herald Sun*, however, criticized the play for its "relentlessly dislikable" characters and for its style, which "flip-flopped" between realism, cartoon, social satire, parody, and contemporary grotesque.[16] Glow writes that a follow-up article in the *Herald Sun* reported that two audience members had walked out at a performance of the play and complained to theatre management.[17] Looking for a response to the complaint, journalist Paul Gray, the writer of the follow-up article, interviewed Ben Ellis, and the director of the play, Tom Healy. Healy stated that the play says some very provocative things about the baby-boomer generation, and that as such, it had the potential to make some audience members angry. Ellis responded that he resists the idea that characters should always be likeable, and explained that this primary concern in writing the play was to illustrate a generational divide that older audience members (and critics) may find confronting.

The mixed reviews of *Falling Petals* raise interesting questions about Richardson's criterion of artistic merit. The theatre reviewers of the *Australian* and the *Herald Sun* answer the question "Does the project succeed aesthetically?" in very different ways. Which reviewer is right? Should assessments of aesthetic merit by theatre reviewers matter to research-informed theatre artists? Are other people's assessments, such as the assessments by the theatre artists a researcher/playwright works with, also important?

The aesthetic merit of *Harriet's House*

Like *Life After George*, *Harriet's House* is written as a naturalistic or realist play and is characterized by the formal elements of realism such as a unified narrative, psychologically plausible characters, and emotional engagement. In Chapter Two, I talked about the writing activities and dramaturgical process I undertook to develop a unified, satisfying storyline, complex, believable characters and dramatic tension. With each of the six drafts I wrote of *Harriet's House*, I responded to feedback that improved the aesthetic merit of the play.

Harriet's House was not reviewed by the media so I cannot provide a theatre critic's assessment of the aesthetic merits of the play or its performance. While such an assessment holds some weight among assessors of research-informed theatre, such as arts funding committees, theatre critics hold their own artistic preferences and often have multiple agendas to meet: their theatre reviews need to sell newspapers. As a playwright, I find the assessment of audience members, particularly those audience members who are experienced theatre artists to be more helpful in reflecting upon the aesthetic merits of my work. Three Canadian playwrights, Beverly Cooper, Marcia Johnson and Melissa Major, have provided me with feedback about *Harriet's House*. Beverly Cooper participated in the reading of the play at the Women's Playwright International Conference in Mumbai. Both Marcia Johnson and Melissa Major participated in the Mumbai reading and saw the play performed at Hart House Theatre.

Cooper (whose play *Innocence Lost* was discussed in chapter one) wrote that the energy in the room during the Mumbai reading was electric. "The dynamic of the family represented in *Harriet's House* felt very real: diverse in its complexities yet universal in the issues all families deal with every day." Cooper reminded me how after the play reading, one of the Indian playwrights spoke up. "She seemed incredulous that you would write about a same-sex couple in such a natural way. For us in Canada, the family dynamic can take so many different forms. *Harriet House* speaks to many issues, yet your play is never preachy: the story and characters always ring true."[18]

Similarly, Marcia Johnson felt that one of the most refreshing things about *Harriet's House* was that it portrayed a lesbian couple as ordinary people trying to manage their way through issues concerning family, community and health. Johnson wrote that in Toronto, lesbians and gay people have generally been portrayed on stage as AIDS victims, drag performers and overtly sexual exhibitionists. For Johnson, *Harriet's House* was a refreshing change. Johnson also commented that the play was accessible to both straight and queer audience members and that the characters, situations and conflicts were engaging and universal.[19]

Melissa Major also found the play to be engaging and commented that *Harriet's House* was a smartly staged play that brought together a multitude of contemporary political and emotional issues. The story never lagged, even through some fairly dramatic setting changes. The text was written in a very conversational way and the actors (both the young actors as well as the more experienced actors) were completely believable.[20]

In addition to the feedback I have received from Cooper, Johnson, and Major, I have received feedback from two other experienced theatre artists working in Toronto: dramaturge Iris Turcott from Factory Theatre and artistic director Brendan Healy from Buddies in Bad Times Theatre. Both Turcott and Healy read *Harriet's House* with a view for production at their theatres. While neither felt that the play was the right project for their own theatres, both believe the play is artistically-shaped. Turcott wrote that *Harriet's House* "is a very heartfelt and intelligent piece of writing and the story is very clearly and simply told." Healy wrote that the play was "a really engrossing read" with "terrific characters and great humanity throughout."

Finally, I have received feedback from the audience of a staged reading of the play at the Mothers at the Margin Conference sponsored by the Australian Motherhood Initiative for Research and Community Involvement (AMIRCI) in April 2011. This feedback is particularly helpful in answering Richardson's question of whether or not *Harriet's House* invites interpretive response.

Interpretative responses from the Mothers at the Margins Conference

The Mothers at the Margins Conference was the Sixth International Conference on Motherhood hosted by the Australian Motherhood Initiative for Research and Community Involvement (AMIRCI). The interdisciplinary conference included keynote addresses on maternal activism, maternal health care during birth, and mothering in contemporary women's writing. It also included sessions on such themes as Aboriginal mothering, fertility and infertility, challenges to mothering, solo mothering, mothering daughters, mothering within violence, and mothering in mixed-race families.

The staged public reading of scenes from *Harriet's House* was scheduled for the end of the first day of the three-day conference. Four colleagues from the Queensland University of Technology (QUT)—Catherine Doherty, Sue Grieshaber, Cushla Kaptizke and Joanne Lampert—my partner Margot Huycke, and Joanne's friend Tori Hadley, performed scenes from the play after one rehearsal. The reading was followed by a twenty-minute discussion. I provided audience members with a feedback form that asked them three sets of questions about the play:

(1) Which moments of the play, if any, resonated with your own experiences of mothering across borders or living together in difference?
(2) Which moments of the play seemed particularly important to you? Why?
(3) Are there other issues, not raised in the play reading today, that are important to address when writing about the experiences of transnational adoptive same-sex families?

An analysis of my notes from the discussion and feedback forms indicate that *Harriet's House* provides multiple entry points into the story and issues facing transnational adoptive same-sex families. For example, in the post-reading discussion, one audience member said she could relate to Harriet's fear of coming out as a lesbian and being abandoned by her Global Family community. She reported that some of the lesbian, gay, bisexual, transgender and queer Aboriginal people she works with have a similar fear. Another audience member, who lives and works in Kerela, India, wrote that although she couldn't find a way to relate to the issues facing Harriet's same-sex family, she connected with Harriet's desire to adopt children living in an orphanage.

> In coming from India, I cannot digest the fact of same-sex families let alone adoption by such families [but an important moment in the play was] when Harriet says children should be adopted by somebody. I sincerely feel that orphans should have a home whether it be by same-sex families or otherwise [Feedback form, Mothers at the Margins conference April 28, 2011].

A third audience member, Australian writer Christina Houen, wrote an interesting response to the question about other issues to address when writing about transnational adoptive same-sex families.

> The father of the Canadian-born child [Clare] seemed to be absent, marginalized. He was mentioned only in the discussion about guardianship, only to be dismissed. Must he be absent/ineffectual/without influence? What if he were a stronger, more present character? Conflict would be increased, issues would be complicated [Signed feedback form, Mothers at the Margins conference April 28, 2011].

Houen's response was connected to her own life experience as a "lost mother" during a time when she was separated from her three young children when their father took them to the United States to live without her prior knowledge or consent. In her own presentation at the Mothers at the Margins conference,

Houen talked about her book *The Lost Mother: a Memoir*. In the abstract of her presentation printed in the conference program, Houen writes:

> After 18 months of legal negotiations I had my first access visit to them, and a second one a year later, before their father brought them and his new stepfamily back to Australia to live. My overwhelming experience of loss was not relieved by the visits; I felt like a missing person, and was lost, not only to my children as mother, but to myself. In the memoir I search back through memories for my lost mother-self, and reconstruct the sense of being absent, not real, on those visits . . . I search for a way of writing the past that affirms what happened, so that it can be willed and released, allowing a rebirth.[21]

The multiple ways the audience members at the conference were able to engage in the reading of *Harriet's House* indicates that the play has the capacity to invite a wide variety of interpretive responses.

Reflexivity in anthropology and creative analytic practice

Richardson's third criterion, "reflexivity" has been discussed in some detail in sociological and anthropological writing about research methodology. In anthropology, the "reflexive turn," like the literary turn described in Chapter One, was a response to a critique of the discipline's complicity with structures of inequality associated with European colonialism. It was also a critique of the idea that anthropologists were objective, neutral observers.

For anthropologists, practicing reflexivity means acknowledging the "situatedness" and partiality of their claims to knowledge. It also means acknowledging their position in relation to the research participants they have worked with. One way anthropologists situate and position themselves is by including some kind of a biographical statement into their ethnographic writing. This statement usually reveals their personal history, the investments they have in their projects, and their relationship to and with their research participants. For example, in her life history project about a Mexican woman street peddler named Esperanza, American anthropologist Ruth Behar situates and positions herself as a "translator" of Esperanza's stories. She translates Esperanza's story from Spanish to English, and she carries Esperanza's stories across the border from Mexico to the United States.

> Without putting down a word on paper, my *comadre* has been writing the story of her life since she was five years old. . . . Yet because it is not in her power to put words to paper, my *comadre* left me the task of putting the words down in this book.[22]

For Behar, the position of anthropological translator is a dangerous position. There is a common practice in Mexico of cutting out the tongue of the snake after one kills it. For if the snake still has its tongue it can talk back from the afterlife and inflict evil. Behar writes, "No doubt about it, this book is a talking serpent."[23] She also writes,

> In telling me her *historias* so I would put them into a book that would talk in the tongue of the *gringos*, Esperanza definitely placed both herself and me in a paradoxical position. In the masked tongue of translation, she hopes she'll be invulnerable to the snakes, only in her original tongue would her confessions be dangerous. But with the border between the United Sates and Mexico, like the border between life and death, being so permeable, can I, no matter how hard I will try, keep guard over this book? How can I be sure it won't return to talk where it shouldn't?[24]

In addition to reflecting upon the danger of her position as the translator of Esperanza's stories, Behar also shares her own life story, and writes about how she met Esperanza in Mexico as she was researching documents from the Mexican colonial inquisition period. Fascinated with both Esperanza and her life story, Behar's initial research focus faded as she began to entertain the project of writing a book about Esperanza's life. Behar is upfront about the privileges she brings to her life history project and the ways in which she is both successful and unsuccessful at negotiating relations of power and privilege as she interviews and writes up both Esperanza's and her own story.

For sociologist Laurel Richardson, reflexivity in creative analytic practice involves several different kinds of considerations. First, Richardson is interested in whether or not, as a research-informed playwright, a writer is familiar with the epistemology of postmodernism.

Epistemology is the branch of philosophy concerned with the nature and scope of knowledge. It takes up questions such as: How is knowledge acquired? What do people know? How do we know what we know? Why do we know what we know? Much of the discussion and debate in the field of epistemology has focused on analyzing the nature of knowledge and how it relates to similar notions, such as truth, belief, and justification. In social science research, common epistemologies are positivist, interpretive, critical, postmodern/poststructuralist.[25] Richardson wants to know if the writer's choice to create research-informed theatre is informed by the epistemology of postmodernism, which, as discussed in Chapter One, doubts that any method or genre can claim to present the whole truth.

Second, Richardson wants to know how a playwright came to write the research-informed play. How did the playwright gather the information embedded in the play? Has the playwright held herself accountable to standards of knowing and writing about the people she has studied? Part of this accountability has to do with how well the playwright has been able to explain how her position as a producer and a product of the play has had an impact on the play. Is there evidence of self-awareness and self-exposure in how the playwright's point of view may have impacted on her telling of the story?

Carolyn Ellis and Art Bochner raise similar questions. Ellis wants to know if a writer has received permission to portray others, and whether those that have been portrayed had an opportunity to contribute their perspectives to the project.[26] Bochner looks for a concern from writers about the people they have written about, and for owning their place in the story they are telling.[27]

While Richardson's first set of questions on epistemology may be of more concern to research-informed playwrights working in the academy, her second set of questions on accountability, ethical practices, position and exposure of point-of-view are helpful for both academics and theatre artists.

Epistemological work in *Harriet's House*

To answer Richardson's question about whether or not my choice to create research-informed theatre is informed in the epistemology of postmodernism, I can point to the capacity of the script to hold together conflicting views on transnational adoption, and to portray multiple realities in the same text. As discussed in Chapter Two, I hope to deepen this capacity by writing a sequel to *Harriet's House*.

Accountability in *Harriet's House*

In answer to Richardson's question of how I have been accountable to what is known about strong qualitative research practice, I can say this: In blending realist, interpretative and dramatic techniques in the creation of *Harriet's House*, I have drawn from multiple sources of knowledge: interviews, personal narratives and documentary films. I have also worked towards crystallization by creating characters that provide and embody multiple perspectives on the issues raised in the research. Finally, I have begun to seek out feedback on how well the play resonates with the experiences of my research participants and other members of adoptive and same-sex families.

One limitation of my research process is that I didn't leave enough time for my research participants to provide me with feedback on the play either before or during the rehearsal period. A good moment for soliciting research participant feedback would have been just before rehearsals began. The cast had not yet begun working with the script, and if changes needed to be made, they could have been made before the team started rehearsing. However, it was not possible to gather the research participants together for a reading of the script before rehearsals. Another possibility would have been to organize a staged reading for research participants during rehearsal period. This would have given research participants and perhaps other members of transnational adoptive families a chance to see how the play was shaping up and an opportunity to voice any concerns they had to the actors and director, as well as to me. However, as will be discussed in Chapter Four, the rehearsal period began late and the actors needed every rehearsal to prepare for the production of the play. So the participants and I agreed that they would come to one of the performances and provide me with feedback then. This arrangement wasn't ideal, and I would not recommend it to my students or other researcher/playwrights. The feedback I received from the play's three performances and one staged reading, however, indicated that I was successful at writing a play that resonated with my participants' lived experiences. Further performances and readings of the play will tease out the ways I might add to and revise the play so that it reflects a diversity of adoptive and same-sex family experiences.

Positioning in *Harriet's House*

In terms of providing evidence of how my point of view may have impacted on my telling of the story of my research, I have provided a set of playwright's notes at the beginning of the script included in Appendix A. Originally, I wrote these notes for the program we distributed for the production of the play at Hart House Theatre.

In these notes, I tell the story of how *Harriet's House* was generated during a trip my partner, Margot Huycke, and I took to Provincetown. In that story I talk about the large number of adoptive same-sex families vacationing in Provincetown, and how comedian Jennie McNulty made that joke about parents travelling from China to Provincetown to look for their children who had been adopted by American lesbian and gay families. *Harriet's House* was created in response to the political tensions I witnessed in Provincetown.

While the program notes provide readers with the understanding that I am interested in how members of adoptive same-sex families negotiate the politics in their everyday lives, they don't explicitly provide them with a particular point of view on transnational adoption. This is because I am not interested in raising or promoting a singular point of view on transnational adoption in *Harriet's House*. I am interested in illustrating the complexities and challenges of adoptive same-sex family life and the kinds of negotiation, rebuilding, and meaning-making family members undertake.

The point of view that does underlie my research and the writing of *Harriet's House* is this: Given the complexity and challenges of living in and working with adoptive and same-sex families, opportunities for discussing these complexities are needed in teacher education classes. While the number of adoptive same-sex families that teachers might work with may be small, discussions of transnational adoptive family life open up discussions about multicultural, multilingual, multiracial family life in general. As a case study of issues facing one kind of contemporary Canadian family, *Harriet's House* has the potential to provoke discussion about the experiences of many other kinds of families with which teachers work.

It is my view of my role as an educator within the critical teacher education movement, then, that seems most salient to highlight in presenting my *Harriet's House* project. This is a position that will be well-known to teachers who read the play in my classes. However, it is a position that was not necessarily known to the audience who came to see the play at Hart House Theatre. A limitation of my playwrights' notes in the program, then, was the absence of any writing about my position as a critical ethnographer and critical teacher educator at the University of Toronto. Some writing about this positionality should be part of future programs that accompany performances of the play. Some writing about how the play was researched, and how it has been informed by the new adoption studies should also be included.

As discussed in Chapter Two, after reading *Harriet's House* or watching a performance of the play, people often ask if my partner Margot and I have adopted children ourselves. Underlying this kind of question is a desire to know how much of my own life story is revealed in *Harriet's House*, and if I am writing from the position of an adoptive mother. A discussion of my positionality as a non-adoptive mother might also be part of future program notes.

Impact

Returning to Richardson's five criteria for creative analytic practice, the fourth criterion asks about impact. Richardson wants to know if a project has affected readers emotionally or intellectually. Has it generated new questions? Has it moved people to write themselves? To try new research practices? Does the project move people to action?

Carolyn Ellis asks similar questions about impact: Does a project help others cope with or better understand their worlds? Is it useful, and if so, for whom? Does it encourage compassion for the characters? Does it promote dialogue? Does it have the potential to stimulate social action?[28] Likewise, Norman Denzin writes that he values projects that "unsettle, criticize, and challenge taken-for-granted, repressed meanings" and "invite moral and ethical dialogue while reflexively clarifying their own moral positions."[29]

The impact of *Harriet's House*

At this moment in the *Harriet's House* project, it is not possible to fully answer Richardson, Ellis and Denzin's questions about impact, as I have not yet mounted a second production of the play or worked with the play within my teacher education classes. However, as discussed earlier, the reading of the play at the Mothers at the Margins conference resulted in a vibrant discussion of the issues presented in the play. In contrast, the reading of the play at the Queer West Festival in August 2010 led to an in-depth discussion of my research and production process. Some members of the Queer West audience were very much interested in writing plays themselves. Similarly, the reading of the play in two different arts-based research methodology courses at the University of Toronto excited several graduate students who have now decided to try writing dramatically. The question of whether or not the play moves people to reflect upon the complexities and challenges of adoptive and same-sex family life will be answered in the next several years, as new audiences and readers engage with *Harriet's House*.

Ability to evoke lived experience

Richardson's last criterion for assessing creative analytic practice, asks whether or not I have been able to present a credible account of the lived experience of transnational adoptive same-sex families. Or, as Carolyn Ellis puts it, if I have been able to demonstrate "authentic adequacy."

Returning to the feedback I received after the performances at Hart House Theatre, there are several aspects of the play that seem to resonate strongly with the experiences of adoptive and same-sex families. They are: Luisa's desire to return to Colombia; Ana's discomfort in Colombia; the fears and negotiations Harriet faces when she comes out as a lesbian in mid-life, and the issues of guardianship raised in the play. As discussed earlier, I plan to continue reading the play in different venues to ask for additional feedback. I am also prepared to continue rewriting the play in response to the feedback I receive. In committing to revising the play in response to future feedback from my audiences, there may be situations where I will not agree with the feedback, and will have to weigh the feedback against the scholarly understanding I have built up over time.

Summing up

Laurel Richardson's criteria for evaluating creative analytic practice emphasizes the aesthetic qualities of a piece of work, as well as its substantive contributions to an area of knowledge. Like Paul Brown, Jim Mienczakowksi and Teresa Moore, Richardson's criteria also point to the importance of establishing an ethical relationship with research participants, and looks for evidence of the practice of reflexivity. Finally, Richardson values projects that encourage or provoke their readers and audiences to critical thought and action. It is a demanding set of criteria that holds research-informed theatre projects to high standards and expectations. In this chapter, I have tried to illustrate how *Harriet's House* tries to meet these standards and have discussed the project's limitations and ways I plan to address them.

Like *Harriet's House*, this book is also a project of creative analytic practice. As a reflective personal narrative of researching, writing and producing the play, the story I present here can also be assessed by Richardson's five criteria. It is not yet possible to assess the book against most of these criteria until it is published, read and discussed by an audience interested in research-informed theatre. However, it is possible to briefly discuss the way in which I have worked towards reflexivity by obtaining feedback on the second draft of this book from two key people involved in the *Harriet's House* project, Jocelyn Wickett and Amy Gullage. Both Jocelyn and Amy read the second draft and commented on the ways my narrative both reflected and did not reflect their own experience of our work together. I made changes to and expanded the narrative in response to their feedback.

In the next chapter of the book, I return to the story of writing and producing *Harriet's House* and discuss what it takes to mount an independent theatre production of a research-informed play script.

· 4 ·

PRODUCING *HARRIET'S HOUSE*

Having located *Harriet's House* in the world of research-informed theatre, and having described the play's development history, my story moves on to a discussion of how Jocelyn, Gillian and I began preparing for the production of the play. While a research-informed script can be powerful, especially when it is read aloud, staging the script with a professionally-trained and experienced artistic team deepens the impact of the research.

I have written the following story of staging *Harriet's House* chronologically, reproducing the steps the team took to mount the play. The story I tell is written from two different perspectives: the perspective of a producer and the perspective of a playwright. Staging *Harriet's House* involved me taking on both roles, as the activities of producing and rehearsing the play overlapped. I begin with the task of finding an appropriate venue for *Harriet's House*.

Finding a venue

Although I did not know it at the time, the task of finding an affordable venue for *Harriet's House* would be more difficult than I had anticipated because of the decision Jocelyn, Gillian and I made to perform the play as part of the Toronto Pride Festival instead of participating in the Toronto Fringe Festival.

The Toronto Fringe Festival provides independent theatre companies from across Canada and around the world with an opportunity to produce their work as part of a two-week theatre festival. For an application fee of $700, each company receives the opportunity to run their show for up to seven performances in either one of the ten official Fringe theatres or in a "Bring Your Own Venue" space. The fee also includes: the assistance of a theatre technician, box office and house management services, publicity through the Festival program, and 100% of the company's box office revenues.

Gailey Road's previous two productions were Fringe shows staged in Bring Your Own Venue spaces. *Pound Predators* was staged at the OISE library, and *Lost Daughter* at The Al Green Theatre in the Miles Nadal Jewish Community Centre (MNJCC). I was fortunate to be able to enter into a community partnership with the MNJCC for our Fringe production of *Lost Daughter*. In addition to a heavily reduced rate on the rental of the theatre, the partnership provided the production with free publicity in the MNJCC's newsletter and on its digital board. However, when I approached the MNJCC about entering into a similar community partnership for *Harriet's House*, the substantially reduced rate that was available for Fringe Festival participants was not available to participants in other festivals and I could not afford to rent The Al Green Theatre at the rate the MNJCC offered. This was a disappointment, as I had already had several promising discussions with Esther Arbeid, the coordinator of theatre partnerships, about producing *Harriet's House* as a MNJCC Pride event. While the MNJCC currently serves a local multicultural community, its historical beginnings as a Jewish recreation centre provides the Centre with close ties to the Jewish community in downtown Toronto. Staging *Harriet's House* at the MNJCC's Al Green Theatre would have given me access to that community in ways that other theatres could not. However, like many other community organizations with theatre spaces, the MNJCC subsidizes their programming with the profits they obtain from renting out their theatre. Savings on the rental of The Al Green Theatre are reserved for particular partnership agreements, like the one the MNJCC has with the Toronto Fringe Festival.

There are other financial advantages associated with producing a show at the Toronto Fringe Festival. For example, the Canadian Actors Equity Association (CAEA) offers waivers to companies producing a Fringe show that allow them to hire unionized CAEA actors at non-unionized rates. These Fringe waivers are not available to companies producing shows at other festivals, like the Pride Festival. However, Jocelyn believed that the Fringe Festival was a space to stage and experiment with new work, rather than present a mature production that had been through a rigorous development process the way *Harriet's House* had been. As well, given the subject matter in *Harriet's House*, both Jocelyn and I were convinced that staging the play as an affiliated Pride event would help build an audience for the show. The Toronto Pride Festival is a two-week event which celebrates life and activism in the city's gay, lesbian, bisexual, transgender and queer communities. I began looking for another venue.

Finding a theatre that was the right size for the audience we expected and that was affordable was difficult. When I discussed the issue with my close colleague and friend Louise Cowin, the Warden of Hart House at the University of Toronto, she said she would see if Hart House Theatre was available for the dates we wanted to perform the show, and determine whether she could come up with an affordable rate for us.

As graduate student Amy Gullage noted, turning to my own relationships and networks at the University of Toronto played a role in finding an affordable space. In fact, it was necessary to turn to my personal relationships and networks many times throughout the production process in order to mount the play. Aspiring writers and producers of research-informed theatre need to create a wide of variety of relationships and networks to support them in the production process.

Hart House Theatre

Hart House Theatre at the University of Toronto opened in November 1919 and was considered a leader in the Canadian "Little Theatre" movement of the 1920s and 1930s. The theatre cultivated and featured some of the country's most acclaimed actors, directors, playwrights and designers of the Pre-World War II era, including Raymond Massey, Dora Mavor Moore, Lloyd Bochner, Lawren Harris, Arthur Lismer, the comedy team of Wayne and Shuster and Merrill Denison. After the war, under the direction of Robert Gill, Hart House Theatre became an extracurricular student theatre and for twenty years provided training for a new generation of Canadian stage professionals: William Hutt, Don Harron, Kate Reid, David Gardner, Arthur Hiller, Donald Sutherland, Norman Jewison and Lorne Michaels. In the 1960s, a third generation of University of Toronto students learned their craft in productions at Hart House Theatre and went on to contribute to a vibrant Canadian theatre scene in the 1970s. Today, Hart House Theatre is still a focal point for the performing arts at the University of Toronto. Every year over a thousand students participate in a variety of drama, dance, music and film projects at the theatre.[1] Staging *Harriet's House* at Hart House Theatre would connect my theatre work to other performance work going on at the University of Toronto, and to an illustrious history. When Louise confirmed that the theatre was available and that she could offer me a rental fee I could afford, Jocelyn, Gillian and I were very excited. While the 450-seat theatre was a larger space than what we needed for our anticipated audience of 150 people each evening, it was designed in such a way that our smaller audience could be seated together in the front rows of theatre where the acoustics were best.

Postponing the production

Unfortunately, as the opening story in the Preface reveals, our production at Hart House Theatre needed to be postponed for a week due to the closure of the University of Toronto during the G20 summit. This postponement had a significant impact on the budget and our plans to attract an audience. Originally we had planned to produce the show during the first weekend of the Pride Festival in order to avoid competing against the Festival's most popular events, which were scheduled to take place during the second weekend of the Festival. The week's postponement not only put us in direct competition with many other Pride events (including the theatre events programmed at Buddies in Bad Times Theatre, Toronto's queer theatre), it also put us in competition with 150 Fringe Festival productions, and the Canada Day long weekend, a weekend during which many of our anticipated audience members had planned to leave the city.

Changing the performance to the second weekend of the Pride Festival also meant changing the days on which our three performances would take place. Originally, we had planned on performing on a Thursday, Friday and Saturday because it was more affordable than performing on a Sunday, when unionized technician fees were higher. A week later, a Thursday performance was no longer as attractive. Thursday was Canada Day, and technician fees were just as high on this statutory holiday as they were on Sunday. Given the uncertainty of attracting an audience on Canada Day, we decided to perform on Friday, Saturday and Sunday. While we managed to attract a respectable audience of 450 to our three performances through innovative changes to our audience development and publicity plans (which are discussed later on in this chapter), financially we didn't break even. As the producer of *Harriet's House*, I ended up spending a large amount of my own money to produce the show. However, it would have been worse if we hadn't taken out insurance on the production.

After considerable research, I had found an insurance policy offered by Mainway Hunter Creighton Incorporated that had been designed especially for theatre producers. Known as Act-One, the policy provides theatre producers with property, crime and liability insurance for a wide variety of circumstances. While the annual fee costs Gailey Road $900, if there is one piece of advice readers should take away from this book, it is this: always insure your production. My Act-One policy covered the difference between the original cost to rent Hart House Theatre and what we ended up paying after rescheduling the production. It also paid for what it cost to produce new publicity materials. The $900 investment was well worth it.

I almost didn't invest in the Act-One policy. As a new producer considering insurance for the first time, I had had difficulty finding a company that specialized in theatre insurance. The first two shows I produced at the Fringe Festival were covered by third party liability insurance provided by the Fringe. The insurance fee came out of my Bring Your Own Venue application fee. At the time I didn't feel the need to take out any additional insurance. When it came time to insure *Harriet's House*, the first insurance policy I bought was not as comprehensive as the Act-One policy. When I finally found out about Act-One, there was a cost to cancelling the policy I had already bought. I talked to my partner, Margot, about the expense of changing to a more comprehensive policy. Having been involved in small business, Margot advised me to make the change. "You can't have too much insurance," she said. "You never know what can go wrong."

Creating a budget and pursuing funding

Every production, whether it is amateur or professional, needs a budget to guide decision-making. As well, most, if not all, grant applications for production funding require a detailed budget. My first draft of the budget for *Harriet's House* was prepared for my grant applications to the Ontario Arts Council and the

Toronto Arts Council. Both Councils have programs that fund independent theatre productions, and I applied to both of them. I also applied for a Pride Access and Diversity grant that was available to participants in the Toronto Pride Festival.

The Arts Council applications required a project description that included the company's mandate, production history and organizational development goals, as well as details of the project. These details included a synopsis of the play, its development history, a list of the members of the artistic team involved in the project, the dates the production was going to take place, and its proposed location. Jocelyn and I also provided an artistic statement about our approach to the play as director and playwright. I also needed to write up a statement about our plans for securing funding for the project, and how we were planning to reach our intended audience. Finally, I provided a timeline for all of the production activities that had to take place in order for us to stage the play. To help me create a timeline I referred to Australian writer Lyn Wallis' book *In Good Company: A Manual for Producing Independent Theatre*.[2] Below are excerpts from my Council grant applications.

Harriet's House: Securing Revenue

> At the current time, *Harriet's House* has been funded by an initial individual donation of $1,000. We have also applied for grant funding from the Toronto Arts Council as well as the Ontario Arts Council. We plan to work at securing sponsorships and partnerships from Toronto's lesbian, gay, bisexual, transgender, and queer communities (e.g., the Gladd Day bookstore, the Parenting Network, the Triangle Program) and allies of Toronto's lgbtq communities (Toronto Women's bookstore, the Elementary Teachers Federation, the Ontario Secondary School Teachers Federation). We anticipate that these sponsorships and partnerships will help us build an audience for *Harriet's House* by promoting our production within their communities and/or buying a set of group tickets to distribute to its members.

Harriet's House: Reaching Our Intended Audience

> Gailey Road's audience base is primarily made up of teachers and academics that are interested in the company's production of women-centred, research-informed theatre. Many of the audience members work at the Ontario Institute of Studies in Education and the Toronto District School Board, and are Tara and Jocelyn's colleagues. In both

of our previous productions, non-educators who were interested in the particular story we were staging expanded our audience base.

We anticipate that *Harriet's House* will attract a lesbian, gay, bisexual, transgender, queer audience. We hope to reach our anticipated audience by staging the play at the beginning of the Toronto Pride Festival, becoming an affiliated event of the Festival, and being included in Pride promotion materials. By staging the play at Hart House Theatre, and being included in their announcements and newsletters, we also hope to attract University of Toronto students taking courses in May and June. Publicity for Harriet's House has already begun. As part of the rental agreement with Hart House Theatre, postcards for Harriet's House have already begun to be inserted in ticket sleeves for all ticket mailouts of events at the venue. Hart House Theatre stages productions of various genres and its own audience base goes beyond students and employees of the university, to include theatergoers all around Toronto.

We also hope to engage the media such as XTRA (Toronto's queer newspaper), Pride FM (Toronto's queer radio station) and CIUT (U of T's radio station) in producing preview pieces of the production that will attract audiences.

Harriet's House: Timeline for Activities

January 2010:

- Sign contract with Hart House Theatre, make box office arrangements.
- Pursue sponsorships and partnerships.
- Hire a graphic artist to design an image for our publicity materials and program.
- Graphic designer designs publicity materials and program.
- Publicity team begins publicizing at U of T talks and events and at queer and allied community events.

February 2010:

- Pursue sponsorships and partnerships.
- Continue publicizing the production at U of T events and queer and allied community events.

March 2010:

- Pursue sponsorships and partnerships.
- Audition call goes out March 1, 2010 and closes March 22, 2010.
- Auditions and casting take place on March 27–28, 2010.
- Continue publicizing the production at U of T events and queer and allied community events.

April 2010:

- Pursue sponsorships and partnerships.
- Pursue preview publicity with XTRA, Pride FM and other Toronto media.
- Begin rehearsals.
- Continue publicizing the production at U of T events and queer and allied community events.

May 2010:

- Pursue sponsorships and partnerships.
- Pursue preview publicity with XTRA, Pride FM and other Toronto media.
- Continue rehearsals.
- Continue publicizing the production at U of T events and queer and allied community events.

June 2010:

- Pursue sponsorships and partnerships.
- Continue rehearsals.
- Continue publicizing the production at U of T events and queer and allied community events.
- Start publicizing on-line, in XTRA and on Pride FM.
- Hold tech-run June 22, 23, 2010.
- Hold performances June 24, 25, 26, 2010.

The preliminary budget I submitted with my applications included the following categories and amounts:

INCOME

Item	Amount
Revenue	
Individual Donation: Tara Goldstein	$1,000.00
Pride Access and Diversity Grant (to be applied for)	$1,000.00
Box office: 10 shares*	
150 tickets × 3 performances = 450 tickets	
450 tickets @ $18.00 = $8,100.00	
($405.00 per share × 10 shares = $4,050.00	$4,050.00
Total:	**$6,050.00**

*Total box office revenue to be divided up between 10 salaries and 10 shares (to offset venue, production and publicity expenses. 10/20 shares will go to artists and 10/20 shares will go to production costs)

EXPENSES

Item	Amount
Venue Costs	$4,943.00
Hart House Theatre Rental	$ 900.00
Ticket Fee ($2 per ticket sold: $2 × 450 tickets = $900)	$5,843.00
Artistic Fees	$250.00
Graphic designer	$250.00
Graphic artist	$800.00 + 1 box office share
Director	$800.00 + 1 box office share
Stage Manager	$ 0 + 1 box office share
Playwright	$ 2,400 + 6 box office shares
Actors (non-unionized) (6 × $400 each)	$4,500.00
Publicity Costs	1/20 box office share
Publicity Assistant	$ 500.00
Poster, flyers, postcards, program, etc.	$ 800.00
Advertising (XTRA)	$ 800.00
Advertising (Pride FM)	$1,200.00
Opening night reception	$ 300.00
Videotaping for archives	$3,700.00
Production Costs	$ 100.00
Lighting designer	$ 300.00
Production designer	$ 750.00
Props/costumes	$ 200.00
Van rental (move in)	$ 200.00
Van rental (move out)	$ 1,550.00
Total:	**$15,593.00**

AMOUNT REQUESTED
$15,593.00 (Expenses) – $6,050.00 (Income) = $9,543.00 (Amount requested)

Applying for Arts Council funding is a very competitive endeavor, and neither one of my grant applications was successful. In his book *So You Want to Be a Producer*, British theatre producer James Seabright writes, "Getting funding behind a project is particularly tough when you're starting out, as you may not have an extensive track record to impress people with and to instill confidence in your ability to deliver the production as planned."[3] However, I did receive $700 from the Pride Access and Diversity Grants program that contributed to our publicity expenses.

Over the development of the production, my preliminary calculation of the production costing about $15,600 had to be modified. As discussed earlier, the rental and technician fees for Hart House Theatre increased when we changed the dates of the production. Three of the actors that we had cast belonged to the Canadian Actors Equity Association (CAEA), and we needed to hire them on CAEA guest artist contracts at Equity rates. Promotion and production design costs were more than I had budgeted for, and because of the competition of other events on the July 1st weekend, we ended up selling more tickets at a promotional price of $10 than we did at the regular price $18.

The final cost of the production was about $23,000 and my individual donation was about $9,000. However, even though *Harriet's House* didn't break even, I still consider the production to be a success. The move to Hart House Theatre gave the artistic team an opportunity to work with unionized technicians. The decision to stage the play as part of the Pride Festival rather than the Fringe Festival gave me the opportunity to arrange guest artist contracts with the CAEA so I could work with unionized actors. As a producer, I matured, and as a company Gailey Road matured as well. While our production of *Harriet's House* lost money and could be considered financially amateur, artistically, it was professional.

Producer James Seabright recommends that every producer's aim should be to follow two basic rules of the game: "Never put your own money into a show, and never put your own money into a show." However, he qualifies this by saying, "The reality is when you're starting out, you may need to stick your neck out a little, because it is very difficult to get other people's money on board to put on a show when you have little or no track record. But this should always be a calculated risk, and within your means."[4]

In addition to grants from government-funded arts councils and trusts and foundation (who distribute private rather than public funds), Seabright suggests that producers also look for corporation sponsorships and donations. The key to obtaining corporate sponsorships is identifying the sort of companies that are most likely to be interested in what your production is about and what you have to offer. Seabright suggests producers think through what it is they can offer a particular company and what sort of amount of money they are looking for in return. He says a typical sponsorship arrangement for a play might involve a number of free tickets to opening night, an advertisement in a program, and a front-of-house display space. Often sponsorships can grow from a personal connection with someone involved with the show.[5]

While I tried to secure a sponsorship arrangement with two local Ontario teacher federations (unions), I was unsuccessful, even though both the federations had committees that were working with lesbian, gay, bisexual, transgender and queer issues in education. Upon reflection, I had not thought through what I could offer the federations in return for their support (they may well have been interested in a front-of-house display space) and I didn't have a personal connection that I could approach. However, if I had used my teaching networks to find a federation connection to pitch my sponsorship request to, I might have been successful. This is a lesson learned for my next production.

I was more successful at securing community sponsorships. The Centre for Urban Schooling at OISE, The Triangle Program at the Toronto District School Board (a high school program for lesbian, gay, bisexual, transgender and queer youth who are not thriving in their local high schools) and a queer community organization called Supporting Our Youth (SOY) all bought tickets to distribute to their members. All three also promoted our production of *Harriet's House* among their networks. In addition to recruiting sponsors for *Harriet's House* I also recruited "supporters" for the play. Like our sponsors, our supporters also agreed to promote the play among their networks. Finally, I was able to find two patrons of the show: Mark and Alix Feldman, the parents of one of our actors, Estée Feldman. After the production was postponed and we lost a substantial number of audience members who couldn't come to the show on the July 1st weekend, the Feldmans bought a large number of tickets for each of our three performances and asked me to distribute the tickets to youth, seniors and artists who would be interested in seeing the show, but couldn't afford to buy a ticket. The Feldmans' generosity and the company's hard work to distribute the subsidized tickets on short notice helped us attract a respectable audience for all three shows.

Putting together an artistic team

With a preliminary budget in place, funding applications completed and sponsorship agreements in progress, the next step was to put together the artistic team that would put *Harriet's House* on stage. Six of the roles were already filled. I was taking on the role of playwright and producer; Jocelyn, the role of director; Gillian, the role of production manager; Lisa Rupchand, the role of graphic designer for our publicity materials and program and Monica Nunes, the role of Assistant Producer. However, we still needed a cast, a stage manager, and a production design team.

The process of putting together a team began with Monica composing an audition call for the actors we needed. As Monica had never written an audition call, I suggested she refer to Lynn Wallis' book on producing independent theatre mentioned earlier. Here is the final draft of the call.

Harriet's House: Hart House Theatre 2010 • Audition Call •

Director: Jocelyn Wickett
Playwright: Tara Goldstein
Produced by: Tara Goldstein/ Gailey Road Productions

Synopsis

Harriet's House dramatizes the story of a Toronto mother with three daughters, two adopted from Colombia, and the challenges they face as they negotiate three family worlds: the world of their own "global family" in Toronto, the world of the adopted daughters' birth country, Colombia, and the new world Harriet, finds herself in when she comes out as a lesbian. Gailey Road is planning to produce *Harriet House* as an affiliated event with the 2010 Toronto Pride Festival.

The play opens with Harriet reluctantly giving her 17-year-old adopted daughter Luisa permission to visit the orphanage in Bogotá where she spent three years of her childhood so that she can find out what happened to her birth mother. While Luisa is in Bogotá, Harriet comes out as a lesbian and introduces her new partner Marty to her two other daughters: 14-year-old Ana, also adopted from Colombia, and 11-year-old Clare, Harriet's birth daughter. Afraid of Luisa's rejection of her new relationship, Harriet doesn't tell her about Marty until Luisa returns home from her visit to the orphanage. Heartbroken that she still hasn't found out what happened to her birth mother, and angry that Harriet didn't tell her about Marty sooner, Luisa returns to Bogotá to continue her search. When Harriet falls seriously ill, however, she decides to travel to Bogotá with Marty, Ana and Clare to bring Luisa back to Toronto.

Characters

HARRIET: A school teacher and mother of three daughters, the first two adopted from Colombia. She ages from 44 to 46.

LUISA: Harriet's eldest daughter, adopted from Colombia at the age of 10. She ages from 17 to 19.

ANA: Harriet's middle daughter, adopted from Colombia at the age of 7. She ages from 14 to 16 .

CLARE: Harriet's youngest daughter, not adopted. She ages from 11 to 13. *We are seeking an actor who is at minimum between the ages of 12 and 14, but can play younger.*

MARTY: A school teacher and Harriet's girlfriend/partner. She ages from 35 to 37.

ANITA: Harriet's friend. Founder of Global Family, an international adoption agency. She ages from 50–52.

Show Information:

Harriet's House will be staged at Hart House Theatre in Toronto from June 24–26, 2010. (Full availability of actors cast will be required from June 23–26 2010). Actors cast in the production will be provided with an honorarium (amount TBA).

Rehearsals

Rehearsals begin in April on Thursday evenings and Sundays at the Ontario Institute for Studies in Education, 252 Bloor Street West, Toronto.

Audition Information and Requirements

Auditions will take place on Saturday March 27 and Sunday March 28, 2010 in Toronto at the Ontario Institute for Studies in Education. Callbacks will be held on Tuesday March 30 and Wednesday March 31, 2010. Please submit a headshot and resume to Gailey Road Productions via email at gaileyroad@gmail.com by March 22nd 2010. For the audition, actors are asked to prepare a one-minute contemporary monologue. Actors may also be requested to do a cold read from the play at the audition.

For more information about Harriet's House and Gailey Road Productions please visit www.gaileyroad.com.

Knowing that it might be difficult to cast *Harriet's House*, we asked Monica to create an extensive list of places to post the audition call. Her final list included professional and community theatre organizations, university theatre programs, high school drama programs, local theatre audition websites, and local arts employment websites.

After two days of auditioning during the last weekend of March, only two of the six roles were cast. Jorie Morrow (cast as Anita) and Julie Burris (cast as Marty) had worked with Gailey Road on our production of *Pound Predators*, and we were really happy to be able to work with them again. We also found our lighting designer, Wade Gamble, and stage manager, Tara Mohan. Dan Parker, who had been part of my small reading group on transnational adoption, joined the team as a sound designer. Dan, who is a musician as well as a high school teacher and student researcher, had lived in Brazil for several years and was excited about composing music for the production. Still missing actors to play Harriet and her three daughters, we sent out a second audition call and held a second set of auditions about two weeks later. Jocelyn's original plan to start rehearsing in mid-April had to be put on hold until all of the roles were filled.

Auditioning actors for the roles of Luisa and Ana brought up issues of race, ethnicity and casting practices for the audition team which was comprised of Jocelyn, Gillian, and me. After the first two days of auditions, the actors that Jocelyn thought were best suited for the roles of Luisa and Ana were not South American or of South American descent. Supinder Wraich identified as South Asian, and Rebecca Applebaum as white and Chinese. While Supinder was fluent in Spanish, Rebecca was not.

The team worked hard to find young actors who were either born in South America or came from families of South American descent, and invited them to audition. Unfortunately, none of these actors was as experienced as Supinder or Rebecca, or as well-suited for the roles of Luisa and Ana.

Before making a final decision about casting Supinder and Rebecca, however, the audition team had a sustained conversation about non-traditional casting for the roles of Luisa and Ana. To guide us in this conversation, we read an article from *American Theatre* entitled "Opening the Golden Gate" written by actor Lily Tung Crystal.[6] In the article, Crystal interviews several casting directors about issues of race, ethnicity and equal representation in theatre. I was particularly interested in the way Leslie Martinson, the casting director of TheatreWorks in Palo Alto, California, talked about the difference between color-blind casting and non-traditional casting:

> Color-blind casting as a phrase is reductive—it implies that someone's cultural context can be set aside. Culture is part of the richness of who we are as human beings. It's usually important to actors in a hundred different ways—why would that not be important on stage? Our commitment is to have the conversation about what role ethnicity plays in a particular production. Sometimes it moves up in import, sometimes down. We're rigorous in examining our assumptions, and I push directors to examine their own (p. 67).

In talking about the role ethnicity played in our production of Harriet's House, the audition team came to the conclusion that while issues of language, culture and race were at the heart of the play, particularly for Luisa who was attempting to reconnect with her cultural heritage in Colombia, it was more important for the actors playing Luisa and Ana to understand the issues at stake than it was for them to identify as Colombian or South American. Supinder and Rebecca were called back to audition together during the second set of auditions. In a discussion of the issues that came up in their audition scene, both actors showed that they had a good understanding of the different views Luisa and Ana held about their linguistic and cultural heritage. Both actors could also relate their characters' beliefs to their own experiences and perspectives. We had found the right actors to play Luisa and Ana, and felt confident about our decision to cast non-traditionally. In the second set of auditions we also found the right actor to play Clare, Esteé Feldman. However, we still hadn't found an actor to play Harriet. We held a third audition call a week later and then a fourth call, the week after that. Just before the fourth audition call was to begin, Jocelyn told the audition team that if we didn't find Harriet that day, we would need to postpone the production, as there wouldn't be enough time to rehearse the show. We were already several weeks behind schedule.

Part of the reason we had such a difficult time finding the right actor to play Harriet had to do with the fact that Harriet comes out as a lesbian in the play. While the actor who played Harriet didn't have to identify as a lesbian, she did have to feel comfortable representing same-sex romance and same-sex desire on stage. Many of the middle-aged actors who auditioned for Harriet were uncomfortable with playing the role of a lesbian on stage. One actor informed us that she could only play the role if she didn't have to kiss another woman on stage. The homophobia that emerged in our auditions for the role of Harriet posed an unanticipated obstacle in our casting process and nearly forced us to postpone the production. On the very last day of auditions Joanne Latimer read for the role of Harriet. She had a terrific audition. We had found our Harriet, and rehearsals started a week later.

Having invested so much time and emotional energy into the production, it was a huge relief to cast Joanne in the role of Harriet. Coming so close to having to postpone the show for another year taught me another lesson: When producing a play with lesbian, gay, bisexual, transgender, queer content, make sure to leave enough time to find actors who can play the roles with passion and authenticity.

Rehearsing: Building strong connections

Rehearsals for *Harriet's House* needed to accommodate the working schedules of one academic who was the Chair of her department, two high school teachers, one social worker, one high school student and four working theatre artists. They took place twice a week, on Thursday evenings and Sunday afternoons, in the large meeting room of my department. A smaller room next door was also available when Jocelyn or the actors needed it. Given the busy schedules of the cast and artistic team, Jocelyn created a rehearsal schedule that made the best use of people's time. As can be seen below, after a first rehearsal with the full cast to begin character development work, she rehearsed the play scene by scene, only calling in the actors needed in each scene. When actors were needed twice in one rehearsal period, but had a break in between the rehearsal of the scenes they were in, they were given review or exploratory work to do in the smaller room.

During the rehearsal process Jocelyn focused on building strong connections among the cast members so that the audience would feel as if they were engaging with an actual family on stage. For example, during the first week of rehearsals, Julie and Estée, the actors playing Marty and Clare, were invited to come to the first rehearsal of scene one so that they could watch Joanne, Supinder and Rebecca, the actors playing Harriet, Luisa and Ana, start building a family dynamic.

Harriet's House Rehearsal Schedule: May 2010

Date	Time	Call for	Main room with Director	Secondary room with support
Thurs. May 6th	5–8	**Character Work**	*Full Cast* Note: wear clothes to move in	
	8–9	**Production/ Designer Meeting**	*Designers and Production Team*	
Sun. May 9th	2–4	**Scene 1**	*Harriet, Luisa, Ana (Anita optional)* Marty and Clare invited to watch to build family dynamic	Open for use
	4–6	**Scene 2**	*Harriet, Marty, Clare, Ana, Luisa*	Open for use
Thurs. May 13th	5–6	**Scene 3**	*Marty, Ana, (Harriet)*	Open for use
	6–7	**Scene 5**	*Clare, Harriet, Luisa*	**Scene 3** *Marty and Ana review*
	7–8	**Family work Or scene review**	*Marty, Harriet, Luisa, Clare, Ana*	
Sun. May 16th	2–4	**Scene 4**	*Harriet, Anita*	*Optional—Ana and Luisa explore scene 6*
	4–6	**Scene 7**	*Ana, Marty, Clare*	**Scene 4** *Harriet and Anita continue*

Thurs. May 20th	5–7:30	**Scene 6**	*Luisa, Ana, Harriet, (Clare)*	Open for use
	7:30–8:15	**Production/ Designer Meeting**	*Production Team and Designers*	Open for use
Sun. May 23rd	2–4	**Scene 9**	*Clare, Harriet, Luisa, Ana, Marty*	Open for use
	4–5	**Scene 10**	*Ana, Luisa*	**Scene 8** *Marty and Harriet explore*
	5–7	**Scene Review (tba)**	*Harriet, Marty, Luisa, Ana, Clare*	Open for use
Thurs. May 27th	5–6:30	**Scene 8**	*Marty, Harriet*	**Scene 6** *Luisa and Ana review*
	6:30–8	**Scene 12 Review Scene 6**	*Luisa, Harriet, Ana, Marty*	Open for use
Sun. May 30th	2–4	**Scene 11**	*Luisa, Anita, (Marty), Harriet*	**Scene 7** *Marty, Ana, Clare review*
	4–5	**Full Team Meeting**	*Full cast, designer, production team*	
	5–6	**Production Meeting**	**Wade not available*	

Jocelyn began the rehearsal process with the fourth draft of the script, which reflected feedback from the four-day workshop, the International Women's Playwright conference and my writing mentor, Sharon Singer. While I was invited to attend all rehearsals, my work as department chair conflicted with many of them. I attended as many as I could. As the actors began working with the fourth draft of the script, they had their own responses to the play and to the lines I had written for their characters. They shared their feedback with Jocelyn, who then approached me about making changes to the script based on the actors' feedback. Working with Jocelyn, I made several changes to the script, and by the end of May, the actors were working with the fifth draft.

In mid-June, just several weeks before the rescheduled show was about to take place, Jocelyn asked me to come to the next rehearsal to talk about why Clare wasn't in the last scene of the play. In the last scene, Harriet and Marty want to get married and ask Luisa and Ana for their support. Harriet also wants Marty to become the girls' guardian if she dies and is seeking the girls' approval. I had originally kept Clare out of the final scene because I thought the talk of Harriet dying and guardianship would be upsetting for her.

After weeks of working to become a family, the cast felt that Harriet and Marty wouldn't have had a talk about guardianship without Clare. I respected their opinion and asked Jocelyn if the actors could improvise the last scene with Clare in it. They did and I heard a variety of things that Clare might say in the scene. So I rewrote the last scene of the play using some of the lines I had heard during the improvisation making sure that they resonated with the research findings. At that same rehearsal, I also asked the cast to help me find a closing image for the play. They improvised several possible visual endings and we found one we liked: Harriet, on her way out to the car to join her family, tidies up the kitchen table, and closes the light. The rewritten scene and the final image appear in the sixth draft of the script, which is the script that was used in the Hart House Theatre run and the script that is included in Appendix A. The collective process we used to make changes to the final scene was a very positive and creative process for me. Making changes to the play during the final set of rehearsals was not difficult because I believed that the changes we made to the final scene made my play a better play. Similarly, moving from my role of producer to my role of playwright back to my role of producer was an intense experience, but a creative and exciting one as well.

Marketing *Harriet's House*

At the same time as Jocelyn, Gillian and I worked to find a venue, pursue funding, put together an artistic team and start rehearsing, I also worked with Monica on the tasks of marketing and publicizing *Harriet's House*. British theatre producer James Seabright makes a distinction between "marketing" and "publicizing" a theatre production. Marketing involves promotions that are paid for, and includes advertising. Publicizing is about securing media coverage, which is cost-free. Media coverage can include news, features and reviews in print, online and broadcast media.[7] While I hadn't read Seabright's book before staging *Harriet's House*, and didn't make the same distinction between our marketing and publicizing activities, I find the distinction very helpful and will use it here as a way of organizing my marketing and public relations story. In his discussion of creating a marketing plan, Seabright offers a comprehensive framework that features four key considerations: Product, Price, Place and Promotion.[8]

Product

As the producer and marketing team begin to design a marketing plan for a show, it is important for them to deeply understand what the show is about and what themes the show explores. Seabright believes that too many marketing campaigns rely on a superficial understanding of what the show is trying to sell. An example of a superficial approach is when a team simply uses the play's synopsis as marketing copy without explaining to potential audience members what might interest them about the show. Another example is when a play's title is very literally represented in the poster design.

Having written *Harriet's House*, I was a producer who deeply understood what the play was about and the themes it explored. *Harriet's House* is a play about a mother raising three daughters, two of whom have been adopted from Colombia. It is also about what happens when the mother comes out as a lesbian in mid-life. The issues the play explores include issues of transnational adoption, homophobia, mothering and daughtering. The marketing copy I wrote to put on the poster, postcards and print advertisement tried to capture these issues: "Love, loss and adoption in a same-sex family. A contemporary drama on mothering and daughtering."

Seabright writes that creating good marketing copy can be a time-consuming process. While it sometimes involves writing a number of drafts, it is important for a producer and the marketing team to get it right. Both the marketing copy and main publicity image are vital sales tools that can make a difference between people deciding to buy a ticket and not buying a ticket.

The main publicity image for *Harriet's House* was designed by graphic designer Lisa Rupchand. In our first attempt to design the image, Lisa and I made the mistake of trying to literally represent the play's title in the poster design by creating an image of a house. Jocelyn, an experienced theatre artist, realized our mistake immediately and asked us to come up with a different image. Our second attempt, which can be seen below and on the cover of this book, was much more sophisticated and eye-catching. Lisa painted two purple, green and yellow trees sitting side-by-side each other with each tree's branches and roots somewhat intertwined. Each tree symbolized one of the two places where Luisa and Ana, Harriet's adopted daughters, were raised. The intertwining of the roots and branches illustrated the multiple roots and connections they had to Toronto and Canada, to Bogotá and Colombia.

While not all graphic designers choose to read the script of the show they are working on, I asked Lisa to do so, and I believe that her reading informed the double tree image that we used in our marketing campaign. Seabright writes that there are four core areas to think about when creating a campaign design: mood (serious, upbeat, funny, youthful); feel (modern, classic, old-fashioned, edgy); colour (bright, somber, clashing, soothing); and style (photographic, illustrative, text-based). Lisa's main publicity image with its brightly coloured, hand-painted trees gave the campaign a youthful mood and a contemporary feel.

Price

Deciding on the basic price for tickets to a production involves making sure that the show's income targets can be met, but that its core audience will not be excluded because tickets are too expensive. Once a basic price for tickets is set, a second decision can be made about how tickets might be discounted to increase sales. Full-price tickets to *Harriet's House* were $18, and discounted tickets for groups of 15 were $10. The week before opening night, in an attempt to increase ticket sales, we also offered a special Pride Festival promotion that allowed audience members to buy $10 tickets at the door on each night of the run.

Place

Thinking about place involves identifying both the right time as well as the right place for a particular show. Given its story about transnational adoption in a same-sex family, we chose to perform *Harriet's House* on the first weekend of the Toronto Pride Festival, not knowing that we would have to postpone the production until the second Pride weekend, and compete with other popular Pride Festival activities.

Seabright suggests that placement in theatre marketing is also about how a show can be introduced to a particular audience in an innovative way.[9] He provides the example of three primetime British television programs that asked its audience to vote for the young actor they wanted to star in *The Sound of Music*, *Oliver!* And *The Wizard of Oz*. In Canada, this marketing innovation was used to cast the role of Maria in a Toronto production of *The Sound of Music* staged by Mirvish Productions in 2008–2009.

Our own introduction of *Harriet's House* was more conventional than innovative. However, it did attempt to reach a large number of people. Early on in our marketing campaign I sent dozens of letters to colleagues, friends and contacts in Toronto's lesbian, gay, bisexual, transgender and queer (lgbtq) community inviting them to promote and/or lend support to the production of *Harriet's House*. I suggested that people could support the show in one of three ways. They could become a "*Harriet House* Supporter" and promote the show through their social networks. They could become a "*Harriet House* Sponsor" and support the play by purchasing blocks of 15 tickets for $10 each, an $8 discount from the regularly priced ticket. They could also become a "*Harriet House* Patron" and make a great contribution to the production by purchasing a quarter of possible house sales (100 seats), a third of house sales (150 seats), or half of possible house sales (225 seats) also at the discounted price of $10. In return for their support, Supporters, Sponsors and Patrons were offered recognition in our program. Additionally, Patrons were also given the opportunity to advertise their organization in the program. My letter writing campaign resulted in twelve Supporters, three Sponsors and two Patrons. As mentioned in chapter two, Mark and Alix Feldman, the parents of Estée Feldman who played the role of Clare, bought 150 tickets over the three-performance run and asked me to distribute them to artists, students, seniors and those who might not be able to afford to come to the show. I distributed the tickets as requested and the Feldmans' support of the show not only resulted in larger houses every night, but helped Gailey Road expand our core audience base.

Promotion

The promotion of a show involves identifying a target audience and then reaching as many of them as possible through a well-thought-out marketing plan. Seabright suggests the plan needs to incorporate an eye-catching campaign design, which can be spread through a mix of advertising in print, online and broadcast media. Advertising should include a set of posters, flyers and/or postcards that can be distributed hand-to-hand, by mail and by e-mail. It can also include special promotions that use niche marketing or gimmicks, and the use of new media to create campaigns that spread the word about a show online.[10]

While Gailey Road's core audience base is primarily made up of teachers, academics and theatre artists who are interested in the company's production of research-informed theatre, the target audience for *Harriet's House* was Toronto's lesbian, gay, bisexual, transgender and queer (lgbtq) community and visitors who were in town for the Pride Festival. To reach our targeted audience, we used our small marketing budget to become an affiliated event of the Toronto Pride Festival, so that a listing of our show would be included in Pride promotion materials. We also decided to place a quarter-page advertisement of the show, featuring Lisa's double tree image, in the Festival's *Pride Guide*. Finally we printed both large posters and small postcards that could be strategically mounted, handed out, mailed and e-mailed. We were able to secure one media sponsor for the show, Shaun Proulx Media. Shaun runs a website featuring upcoming and current lgbtq events in Toronto. He advertised *Harriet's House* by giving away free tickets to the show.

In thinking about ways of improving our marketing planning for our next production, James Seabright's suggestion of identifying other shows with the same target audience and looking at the ways they spend their marketing budgets is helpful. Seabright provides a list of questions to focus on when analyzing the marketing campaign of other productions:

- Which publications do they advertise in?
- What size are their advertisements and where are they positioned? Do they share the page with other ads or only with editorial content?

- How does their poster image look, both in print and on the web, and how does it relate to the production itself in terms of feel and design?
- What does their show sound like based on its marketing copy, and how does this vary from the experience of seeing the production itself?
- To what extent are they using online marketing, and how big a part of the campaign is it?
- How are their tickets priced, and what is their performance schedule?[11]

Publicizing *Harriet's House*

While Monica and I worked on our marketing campaign, we also worked on publicizing *Harriet's House* by trying to secure media coverage. Of all the different aspects of staging *Harriet's House*, this was the aspect at which we were the least successful. Although we produced professional-looking press packages and sent them to people writing about new theatre productions in Toronto, the timing of *Harriet's House* during the first weekend of the Toronto Fringe Festival meant we were competing with many other more established theatre companies.

Seabright writes that an ideal public relations campaign is driven by a proactive publicist who is able to secure good media coverage. Since our small marketing and public relations budget did not allow us to hire an experienced publicist, Monica and I took on this role ourselves. However, without an experienced publicist working on the project, our press packages did not result in provoking media interest in the show.

Seabright understands that producers, especially those who are new to producing, may need to be their own publicist since hiring an experienced publicist can be expensive. However, he suggests that not having the budget available to hire a publicist shouldn't stop producers from exploring possibilities. Sometimes, he writes, well-established publicists will work on an interesting project or for a promising producer for a little or no money. However, even if such an offer doesn't materialize, it is still worth meeting with a few experienced publicists to learn about the possible angles and approaches that can be used to get coverage for a particular show. In the final analysis, however, Seabright writes that even when armed with the best ideas imaginable, a producer will not have the same influence as an experienced publicist in terms of getting the attention of the media.

About a week before *Harriet's House* was to open, my brother Carl Goldstein, a film director and producer in Los Angeles, e-mailed to ask how the production was going. I told him about our lack of media coverage, and he generously took on the role of publicist. Experienced in the world of film production, Carl managed to get *Harriet's House* coverage from two well-known Toronto entertainment newspapers: *Now Magazine* and *Eye Weekly* just days before opening night. His stunning last-minute success underscores Seabright's point about finding room in the overall production budget to hire an expert. To recruit the right publicist, he suggests asking for recommendations from fellow producers.

Returning to the topic of press kits that were briefly mentioned earlier, the press kit for *Harriet's House* contained a press release that the media could use to release information about *Harriet's House* to the public, a synopsis of the play, biographies of the actors and artistic team, and a history of the company. When putting together a press kit, it is important to remember that marketing copy for posters, flyers and brochures need to be distinctly different from copy prepared for a press release. While marketing copy is written for a ticket-buying audience, a press release is written for journalists and broadcasters. Seabright suggests that the media is more interested in a show's "features" while a potential audience is more interested in a show's "benefits." Here are a few examples of what the media copy and marketing copy or *Harriet's House* might look like:

Feature (media copy)	**Benefit (marketing copy)**
The latest play from award-winning playwright Tara Goldstein.	A "heartfelt and intelligent play" (Iris Turcott, Factory Theatre) with "terrific characters and great humanity" (Brendan Healy, Buddies in Bad Times).
Sound designed by Dan Parker, rock musician and front man for the Québécois rock group FP2.	Music performed and recorded by Québécois rock musician Dan Parker using only his voice.
Ensemble led by Joanne Latimer (*Me and Luke*) and Supinder Wraich (CBC's *The Border*)	The cast of six women is led by popular Canadian television actors Joanne Latimer and Supinder Wraich.

As explained by James Seabright, a show's "features" are usually what someone within the theatre and entertainment world would think about mentioning first. A show's "benefits" describe what the audience will gain from seeing the show. When writing marketing copy, Seabright suggests not using too many superlatives:

> Anything which claims to be "hilarious," "unforgettable" or "life-changing" is almost certainly not going to live up to its own hype. There is a fine line between enthusiasm and exaggeration, which modern consumers can spot instantly. Just one over-the-top claim can make the whole pitch seem doubtful in the eyes of the reader.[12]

Seabright also suggests using positive press quotes about the show or about previous work by the people involved in the show, as they offer third-party validation of your claims. While I do not have any press quotes about *Harriet's House* because it has not yet been reviewed by the media, I do have positive quotes from well-known Toronto theatre artists who have read the script. These quotes appear in the first example of "benefits" above.

In the first example in the "features" column, I mention that I am an award-winning playwright. I won the Canadian Jewish Playwriting award in 2005 for my play *Lost Daughter* which is briefly described in Chapter One. Seabright suggests that references to awards are always more effective when they refer to the production, rather than just someone who is involved with it and who won an award for something else. However, in absence of any awards for a particular production, my own view is that it is best to use what you have got.

One thing that Seabright suggests excluding in the marketing copy is a "call to action," such as "Buy your tickets now by calling . . ." or "Be sure to book your tickets now to avoid disappointment." While a venue brochure or website might have its own focused appeal for people to buy tickets immediately (the Hart House Theatre website had such an appeal for all the shows it staged in 2010), Seabright believes it becomes boring if each and every show listed implores the reader to book right away. As a final piece of advice on writing copy, James Seabright suggests that producers ask several people who aren't involved with the production to take a look at their marketing and media copy. Feedback from outsiders can help producers ensure that the features and benefits of the show are being clearly conveyed.

Performing *Harriet's House*

As mentioned in the Preface, our three performances of *Harriet's House* at Hart House Theatre attracted a total of 450 people. While we were not able to get any media reviews of the show, we did receive feedback from many of our audience members. Given that *Harriet's House* is a research-informed theatre project, I was particularly interested in whether or not the issues presented in the play resonated with adoptive families and same-sex families. The initial feedback we received suggested I had been successful in taking the issues I had researched and putting them on stage. While planning the production of *Harriet's House* at Hart House Theatre I received an invitation from Jaclyn Isen to produce a staged reading of the play for the annual Queer West Festival held in Toronto in August. All six members of the cast were available to perform at the reading and participate in the discussion that followed it. Once again, I was particularly interested in feedback from members of adoptive families and same-sex families. However, at the Queer West reading there was a lot more discussion of the process I undertook to write and stage *Harriet's House* than there was about the issues the play presented. While the impact of a staged reading is not as strong as the impact of a performance (which has lights, music and a set to layer the themes of the play), the advantage of a reading of is that is portable.

After one set of staged performances and one staged reading, I still consider *Harriet's House* to be a work-in-progress that will be subject to changes based on the feedback I continue to receive about the play. The script included in Appendix A is the script we used for our production at Hart House Theatre in 2010; however, it is possible that future drafts of the script may be different from this first production script.

As I begin to close this chapter on producing research-informed theatre, I offer up a list of ten lessons I learned from mounting *Harriet's House*.

1. Write up job descriptions for everyone on the artistic team, and provide each member of the team with a contract that describes what is expected of them on this production.
2. Make sure to leave enough time to find actors who can play gay, lesbian, bisexual, transgender, and queer roles with passion and authenticity.
3. Make sure that there is enough time set aside for research participants to hear a reading of the play either before or during the rehearsal period.
4. Discuss what kind of theatre (in terms of size, intimacy, location, and cost) is most appropriate for the production.
5. Create funding, marketing, publicity and production work plans right from the beginning of the project. Work with new and established networks to secure sponsors for the production.
6. Budget for and then hire a publicist.
7. Discuss in advance what roles the producer, director and production manager will play around set, costume, light, and sound design

activities, and discuss when production meetings will be scheduled and when the designers can have access to the director and the cast.

8. Order vans and trucks for moving the set into and out of the theatre as early as possible.
9. Order more programs than you think you will need.
10. Ask everyone on the artistic team and their networks about connections they have to media contacts so that you can get the show reviewed.

Growing Gailey Road

Despite some worry and disappointment during the production process, the ultimate success and exhilaration of producing *Harriet's House* took me to a new moment in my work with research-informed theatre. As mentioned in Chapter Two, audience members wanted to know what happens to Harriet's family, and I have decided to write about Luisa, Ana and Clare's experiences, as they grow older. Getting a sequel to *Harriet's House* on stage, however, will require funding and planning.

In the fall of 2010, I approached Holland Hendrix, OISE's new Advancement Officer, and asked him if he would provide me with some mentorship around developing a strategic five-year plan for Gailey Road Productions. He agreed. I told Holland that the primary development goal for the company in the next five years was to establish a strong financial base so we could continue to develop, produce and perhaps even tour work from the *Harriet's House* project. Holland suggested that in addition to applying for arts council funding like we did for *Harriet's House*, Gailey Road also needed to apply for private foundation funding, to develop a donor prospect pool and to create a major gifts program. Doing so required creating a Board of Directors. This was the same advice I had received from Toronto-based theatre producer, Derrick Chua.

I needed to do some serious thinking about whether or not I was ready to grow Gailey Road Productions in the way that Holland and Derrick suggested. While I had learned a lot and gained some skills in theatre production by staging *Harriet's House*, creating a Board of Directors for Gailey Road took me out of my comfort zone. So did engaging in fundraising beyond arts council grant writing. However, I believed that if I wanted to see my research-informed plays performed and discussed outside as well as within my own classrooms,

I needed to move forward. So I invited three colleagues, each with a different set of experiences, skills and networks, to join Gailey Road's first Board of Directors.

Bessie Giannikos, who is the Business Officer in my department, has accounting and strategic planning expertise. Julie Kerekes, a faculty member in my department, has a personal interest in supporting the *Harriet House* project, as she is an adoptive mother herself. Having Julie on the Board links Gailey Road to adoptive family communities both in and beyond Toronto. Finally, Jeffrey White is a teacher with The Triangle Program at the Toronto District Board of Education who supported the production of *Harriet's House* by becoming a Community Sponsor for the production. As a Community Sponsor, The Triangle Program bought a set of group tickets, which helped us build a healthy audience for the run. Having Jeffrey on the Board links Gailey Road to lesbian, gay, bisexual, transgender and queer youth and the communities who support them. Gailey Road held its first board meeting and constituted its first Board of Directors on December 13, 2010. Jeffrey White became the Chair of the board, Bessie Giannikos, the Treasurer, and Julie Kerekes, the Secretary.

In the next five years, we will see if the company is able to develop and produce further work from the *Harriet's House* project. If it is not possible to raise enough money to produce work from the project, *Harriet's House* and its sequel can still be used in classrooms, schools and conferences to provoke critical discussions on issues facing transnational adopted youth, their families and their teachers. There are two ways to do this. The first is to ask students and conference participants to participate in a cold reading of the script. The second is to rehearse and present a staged reading of the play, like the reading that was presented at the Mothers on the Margins conference.

Summing up

As a critical ethnographer, it has been exciting for me to move from writing traditional critical ethnographies to writing and producing performed ethnographies and research-informed theatre. I have been fortunate to be researching and writing at a time when there is institutional support for such work. My research program on performed ethnography and research-informed theatre is respected in my department and at OISE, and I have recently received a Social

Sciences and Humanities Research Council (SSHRC) Grant to research the impact my work of *Harriet's House* has had on teacher education. At a time when government funding of the arts has been cut deeply, and theatres are forced to place commercial viability above other considerations when producing a new play, my work with research-informed theatre could never have developed the way it has without the institutional support of my university. My colleagues at OISE have been extremely encouraging of my work, and have attended staged readings and performances of my plays over the past twelve years. Finally, I have benefited immensely from the work of other scholars such as Norman Denzin, Yvonne Lincoln, Laurel Richardson, Ron Pelias and Bud Goodall, who through their own research-informed creative writing projects, as well as their support for such projects, have opened the door for other researchers like myself to write creatively.[13] Conferences such as the International Qualitative Research Conference held annually at the University of Illinois, Urbana-Champagne, and journals such as *Qualitative Inquiry*, *The International Journal of Curriculum and Pedagogy* and *Teaching Education Journal* have provided me with spaces in which publish and discuss my research-informed theatre work with other researchers and teacher educators. The future of such work depends on continued institutional support and opportunities for both undergraduate and graduate students to learn how to engage with the literary turn in ethnography and other social science research. I hope that this book provides such an opportunity. In the next and final chapter of the book, I answer a set of questions that I am often asked about research-informed theatre in general, and about the writing and production of *Harriet's House* in particular.

· 5 ·

QUESTIONS AND ANSWERS ABOUT *HARRIET'S HOUSE*, RESEARCH-INFORMED THEATRE AND ARTS-BASED RESEARCH

Over the five years that I have been working on *Harriet's House*, I have been asked a number of questions about the project. I have also been asked a number of questions about research-informed theatre and arts-based research more generally. In this last chapter on writing and producing *Harriet's House* I answer some of these questions, expanding on and layering some of the discussions that have been taken up in the previous chapters.

1. How did you find a creative team to workshop *Harriet's House*?

Finding a creative team involves networking, good will, collaboration, asking for help and reciprocity. As discussed in Chapter Two, *Harriet's House* is the third play that my theatre company Gailey Road Productions has produced for the stage. There are three core members of the company. I am the Founding Director and one of the company's two Artistic Directors. Jocelyn Wickett is the other Artistic Director and Gillian Lewis is the Production Manager. The three of us planned the *Harriet's House* workshop together and took on the roles of playwright (me), director (Jocelyn) and workshop manager (Gillian). As can be seen in their biographies included in Appendix B, Jocelyn and Gillian are professionally-trained theatre artists. Through their professional training, they have cultivated a network of theatre artists they enjoy working with. Likewise, as a playwright and academic, I have begun to cultivate a network of theatre artists, graduate students and colleagues interested in research-informed theatre and arts-based research. I have also been able to meet theatre artists through auditions for productions of my plays, and through my work as Chair of the Women's Caucus for the Playwright's Guild of Canada.

The first step for researcher-playwrights who want to put together a workshop is to find a theatre director to design and facilitate the workshop. The director will have his or her own network of theatre artists to help you explore the story, characters, themes and politics of your script. Jocelyn Wickett was one of my teacher education students at OISE. The year we met, she was enrolled in the Bachelor of Education program to credential as a high school drama teacher. Some researcher-playwrights may be ready to facilitate the workshop themselves, and will only need to find a group of actors who are well-suited to working on the project.

Researchers who do not have any contacts within the theatre world at all need to cultivate a network of theatre artists with whom they can collaborate. For example, Ross Gray, a health researcher from the University of Toronto, contacted Ryerson University's Act Two theatre program and asked them to workshop and stage productions of his research-informed play script on breast cancer.[1] Act Two is a continuing education/community theatre program for actors 55 years and older, and the actors volunteered their time to the project.

While it is not typical to have an ethnographer join a play development workshop, I asked OISE graduate student Amy Gullage to document the workshop activities and interview me at the end of each workshop day. Having written *Harriet's House* as a research-informed play script, I wanted to document the ways in which the script evolved incrementally through the workshop process. I also wanted to make sure that the dramatic changes I made still resonated with the research I had undertaken to write the script. Having been part of my research group on transnational adoption and same-sex families, Amy was an ideal person to do this work.

2. What did you do during the workshop?

As mentioned in Chapter Two, three questions guided Jocelyn's design of the workshop:

1. What insights do the actors have about each of the characters based on their first reading of the play?

2. What new insights emerge when the actors explore the dialogue and voice of each of the characters?
3. What new scenes might be written to incorporate the insights that emerge in the workshop?

To answer these questions, Jocelyn's workshop began with a focus on the whole play, then moved to a focus on individual scenes. She ended with explorations of possible new scenes that had not yet been written.

Schedule for Harriet's House Workshop

	Monday	Tuesday	Wednesday	Thursday
9:30–10:00		*Room available for individual warm up*		
10:00–12:00	Introductions Overview Community building	Scene Work (table/on feet/ improv)	Scene Work (table/on feet/ improv)	Scene Work (table/on feet/ improv)
12:00–1:00		*Lunch provided*		
1:00–4:00	Script Reading *focus on whole play	Scene Work (table/on feet/ improv)	Scene Work (table/on feet/ improv)	Improvisation Final writing and reflection
4:00–5:00	Tara's interview with Amy	Tara's interview with Amy	Tara's interview with Amy	Tara's interview with Amy

On the first day of the workshop, we began the overview activity with Jocelyn asking me to answer several questions about the play: Why did you write the play? What do you want the play to say? What hopes do you have for the play? What concerns do you have about the play? In asking a question of what I want the play to say, Jocelyn was asking about the ways I wanted to answer the research questions I had posed about transnationally adoptive same-sex families. In asking about concerns, she gave me the opportunity to discuss a number of ethical issues that come up when writing a research-informed play script.

Some of what I said about the play in response to Jocelyn's questions has been discussed in Chapter Two. However, in listening once again to my introduction of the play, which was audiotaped, I realize that I spent a lot of time talking about how I was interested in staging the complexities and challenges of adoptive same-sex family life, something I discuss in Chapter Three.

After I had answered Jocelyn's questions about the play, Jocelyn led us in a community-building activity to help us build a preliminary connection to one another before beginning the first reading of the play. We continued getting to know one another during lunch, and after lunch, we did a read-through of the entire play. For the first read-through, Jocelyn assigned a role to each of the actors to read, giving Jorie Morrow two roles to read, Anita, and Clare, who are never in the same scene. I read the stage directions and Gillian timed all the scenes so we would know how long the play was. The read-through was followed by a discussion that gave the actors an opportunity to share their own first responses to the play. After this discussion, Jocelyn asked the actors to list what they already knew about each of the characters in the play, and what they wanted to know. These lists gave me the opportunity to think about ways in which the characters in the play could be further developed.

On the second and third days of the workshop, as well as on the fourth morning, Jocelyn moved us into a reading and discussion of each scene of the play. The actors played different roles in these scene readings so I could see how different actors interpreted different moments in the play. Jocelyn then asked the actors to read parts of a scene "on their feet" showing me how the words I had written might be staged and embodied on stage by the actors. As discussed in Chapter Two, sometimes Jocelyn would ask the actors to improvise a moment in the scene or a moment before and after a scene. These improvisations provided me with ideas on how to improve or nuance my dialogue. Actors who were not reading a role in a particular scene were asked to listen to the reading carefully and participate in the follow-up discussion. As also discussed in Chapter Two, the discussions focused on what the actors felt in the scenes they were reading, the lines that were not clear to them, the lines they felt their characters would not say, and the lines that were too wordy and could be edited for more dramatic effect. There was also discussion of the timeline of the play and what the audience needed to know about Harriet's family to better understand a dramatic moment or a particular scene.

On the last afternoon of the workshop, Jocelyn asked the actors to improvise several new scenes that had not been written into the play. These included a scene that had Marty moving into Harriet's house, and a scene that had the family saying goodbye to Luisa just before she left for Colombia. The purpose of these improvisations was to give me an opportunity to see if I wanted to write any new scenes for the play that would layer or deepen the storyline or characters. I found the improvisation of Marty moving into Harriet's house particularly powerful for the way it established a new connection between Marty and Ana and Clare, and I wrote that scene into the next draft of the script.

In choosing which new scenes to improvise, Jocelyn and I returned to our workshop discussion of the play's timeline and asked ourselves what events might have happened in between the scenes that had already been written.

We then talked about what these events might have sounded like, whether or not they would be interesting and dramatic to stage, and whether or not they would help the audience better connect to characters' journeys in the play. The scene of Marty moving into Harriet's house was a scene that was both dramatic to stage and helped the audience to understand what that moment was like for Marty, Ana and Clare.

The workshop ended with Jocelyn asking the actors to write out the answers to the following questions: If you could change one thing about the play what would it be? Why? If you could tell Tara to keep one moment / scene what would it be? Why? What are some questions the play raises for you? What character did you feel most drawn to? Least? Why? In terms of process, what aspects worked for you? What process suggestions might you have for next time? I used the answers to the questions about the play to help me make decisions about what revisions I wanted to undertake. The answers to the questions about process will be helpful for the workshop we are planning for *Ana's Shadow*.

After such a rich and engaged workshop, it was a challenge to decide what I wanted to revise and what I did not. As mentioned in Chapter Two, I had covered four copies of the script (one for each day of the workshop) with notes. I decided that I needed time to think about the numerous discussions and improvisations I had heard and seen, so I created a chart for documenting the feedback I had received. The chart had three columns: "Revise," "Think About Revising," and "Don't Revise for Now."

As also mentioned in Chapter Two, after each workshop ended, Amy Gullage interviewed me about the day's activities. Amy's questions asked me about my initial reactions to the day's work: what surprised me; what brought me joy; what disappointed me; what inspired me and what revisions I was considering. Amy's questions helped me articulate which parts of the day resonated most and also helped me think about revisions.

While I engaged in a creative and collaborative workshop with the director and artists to further explore and deepen the draft of the play, the script was not written or conceived through collective creation. In the end, I was the one who considered all the work and discoveries from the workshop, made decisions, and revised the draft so it would be ready for production.

3. Is it necessary to establish your own theatre company to produce research-informed theatre? How did Gailey Road Productions begin?

There are a number of ways playwrights get their research-informed scripts produced for a public audience. Some playwrights have an on-going relationship with a professional theatre in their community which is interested in producing their work. As mentioned in Chapter One, all of the Australian verbatim plays discussed by Paul Brown were produced by professional theatres in Melbourne and Sydney. Other playwrights submit their work to professional theatres whose mandate matches the subject of the play they have written, hoping to interest them in producing their work. Still other playwrights work with community theatre groups to stage their work. As mentioned earlier, in the answer to question one, Toronto health researcher and playwright Ross Gray collaborated with Ryerson University's Act Two community theatre program to workshop and stage productions of his research-informed play script on breast cancer. On the other hand, playwrights like Moisés Kaufman and Alistair Newton, whose work was discussed in Chapter One, establish their own theatre companies to produce their projects.

I decided to create my own theatre company after several years of submitting my plays to professional theatre companies and not having any success in getting any of them produced for a public audience. Gailey Road Productions was established in 2007 so I could produce my play *Pound Predators* as part of the Toronto Fringe Festival. For that first production, I participated in the Bring Your Own Venue program and used the ground floor of the library at OISE to perform the play. It was an excellent way to begin learning how to produce my own work. The following year, I participated in the Fringe Festival's Bring Your Own Venue program once again, but was able to produce my play *Lost Daughter* at the Al Green Theatre at the Miles Nadal Jewish Community Centre (JCC). As discussed in Chapter One, the JCC had a partnership program that provided professional theatre space to Fringe-affiliated shows at a reduced rate. Two years later, after saving money to produce *Harriet's House* as part of the Toronto Pride Festival, I was able to stage my work at Hart House Theatre, a theatre that employed unionized technicians. Each production provided the company with the opportunity to professionalize just a little bit more. *Pound Predators* was produced in a community space. *Lost Daughter* was produced in a professional theatre space and featured one unionized actor. *Harriet's House* featured three unionized actors and was produced in a unionized theatre space. As discussed in Chapter Four, for Gailey Road Productions to continue to grow as an independent theatre company, it needs to apply for private foundation funding, develop a donor prospect pool, and create a major gifts program. This requires creating a Board of Directors and applying for a charitable registration number, which I did in December 2010.

Not all research-informed playwrights will want or need to create their own theatre companies to produce their work for a public audience. Creating my own theatre company was exciting for me, and provided me with opportunities to publicly share my work in ways I could not have done without having self-produced it.

4. How do I begin to submit my work to professional theatres and interest them in producing my work?

A good way to begin is by making a list of the theatres you think would be interested in producing your play. Research the kinds of seasons the theatres in your community produce, and see if your play is a good match for any of them. Also, research theatres located outside your community. An excellent American resource for putting together such a list is *The Dramatist's Sourcebook* compiled by the Theatre Communications Group (if you consult this book, make sure you use the latest edition).[2] The second step is to send out "inquiry letters" to each of the theatres on the list. These letters should include a short synopsis of the play and a brief synopsis of its development and production history. Most playwrights do not send a copy of their script or a sample of their script along with their inquiry letter, unless they are asked to do so. Letters of inquiry often need to be followed up. If I do not hear from a theatre company within six months, I write and ask if they have had an opportunity to read my inquiry letter. Playwright researchers who have several scripts ready for production submit them to theatres, contests and journals regularly. Some writers I know research and write creatively for three weeks every month and then spend the fourth week sending their work out. This process requires both confidence in your writing and emotional resilience. Often this resilience comes from a deep commitment to seeing particular projects staged for a public audience.

5. What can you tell me about other arts-based research practices?

To answer this question, I will turn to Patricia Leavy's recent book *Method Meets Art: Arts-Based Research Practice*.[3] While there have been several useful arts-based research methodology texts published in the last few years, including Gary Knowles and Ardra Coles' *Handbook of the Arts in Qualitative Research: Perspectives, Methodologies, Examples, and Issues*,[4] Leavy's book is a well-written, accessible introduction to six kinds of arts-based research practices: narrative inquiry, poetry, music, performance, dance, and visual art.

The book reviews how each practice has developed, the way the practice has varied, the kinds of research questions the practice can address, and examples of studies that have been conducted with the practice. The book also includes annotated lists of journals, and websites and recommended readings to assist researchers who want to use one of the six practices, or a combination of practices, in their research.

Leavy defines arts-based research practices as a set of methodological tools that can be used by qualitative researchers during all phases of social research, including data collection, analysis, interpretation, and representation. This definition aptly describes my work with *Harriet's House*, which used documentary films and personal narratives, as well as interviews to research adoptive same-sex families and creative play writing practices to interpret and represent research findings.

In her review of the field, Leavy writes that arts-based methods have drawn on practices of literary writing, music, performance, dance, visual art, film and other media to produce short narratives, novels, experimental writing forms, poems, collages, paintings, drawings, performance scripts, theatre performances, dances, documentaries, and songs. While each of these practices and texts is quite different from the other, what they have in common is their ability to draw on the arts' potential to be "emotionally and politically evocative, captivating, aesthetically powerful and moving."[5] These qualities can be harnessed by researchers to explore topics that are hard to represent, such as love, death, power, memory, fear, loss, desire, hope and suffering.[6] They can also be harnessed to promote dialogue and facilitate conversation. As Leavy writes, "The arts ideally evoke emotional responses, and so the dialogue sparked by arts-based practices is highly engaged."[7]

6. Is it necessary to train as an artist before undertaking an arts-based research study?

There is a range of interesting answers to this question. As discussed in Chapter One, health researcher/playwrights Jim Mienczakowski and Teresa Moore believe that ethnodrama is different from traditional theatrical work. They see it as a new aesthetic that values the accurate interpretation of research findings over the style, mode, and traditions of theatrical presentation.[8] For Mienczakowski and Moore, formal training as a playwright is not as important as a playwright's commitment to letting the research participants do the talking.

However, as discussed in Chapter Three, Laurel Richardson includes aesthetic merit in her five criteria for creative analytic practice, and argues that such practice requires researchers to meet another standard, a standard of artistic excellence. Richardson writes that creative writing is a skill that can be developed through reading, courses, workshops and practice, and provides a set of writing practice exercises at the end of her article *Writing: A Method of Inquiry*.[9] Similarly, Patricia Leavy writes that arts-based researchers need to pay attention to the artistic craft they are adapting and learn the rules and the tradition they are borrowing from. For example, researchers should not assume that they can "dabble" in poetry, without any research into the discipline itself.[10] While some researchers (like me) have pursued artistic training themselves, others have worked in cross-disciplinary collaborations with artists to strengthen the aesthetic dimension of their research. For example, my colleague Heather Sykes collaborated with theatre artists Anne Swedberg and Jennifer Chapman to create *Wearing the Secret Out*, a performed ethnography that dramatizes Sykes' life-history research about lesbian physical education teachers.[11]

Education researcher Carl Leggo at the University of British Columbia believes that while arts-based research texts must be created with due consideration to aesthetic merit, audiences need to realize that these texts are not only artistic representations, they are also research texts. For Leggo, the question that should be asked when evaluating arts-based research is not "Is this good arts-based research?" but "What is this arts-based research good for?" Aesthetic evaluation should be based on the value of the work in terms of research and pedagogical functions.[12] A similar stance can be seen in Richardson's criterion of substantive contribution.

For researchers who decide to pursue some kind of artistic training or professional development, it is important to think about what kind of skills you need and what kind of training will serve your work well. For example, at Spalding University, I was educated in the genre of naturalist/realist drama that is often produced in mainstream theatres. While this kind of training has served me well in developing many of my research-informed playwriting projects, I know that additional professional development in other genres, such as feminist theatre, or biography theatre, for example, will be helpful for other projects.

For some researchers, the idea of developing skills as a creative writer or artist is intimidating. The idea that that artists are born, not made, prevents them from developing the artistic skills they need to engage in arts-based research projects. However, the story of my own growth as a playwright shows that it is possible to think of playwriting as a craft that can be developed by pursuing some initial training, getting feedback on scripts, and revising scripts until they are strong enough to present to an audience.

7. What did you take away from your experience of completing a Master of Fine Arts degree in playwriting at Spalding University?

One of the most important things that I took away from my experience at Spalding was learning how to make time for my playwriting. The four-semester program was a brief-residency program that brought its students to Spalding for a ten-day residency each semester. After the residency, students were set up with a mentor to work on a variety of assignments and projects one-on-one for the rest of the semester. Like many other students, I was working full-time while I was enrolled in the program. Ideally, our instructors expected us to spend about twenty-five hours a week reading and writing. In the first two semesters, there were short essays to write on the craft of playwriting as well as playwriting projects. In the third semester, there was a longer academic essay to write, and in the fourth and final semester, a creative thesis. To complete all of my assignments, I had to learn how to make my playwriting a top priority.

Writing the academic essays in semesters one, two and three gave me an opportunity to engage in the study of playwriting craft. For example, in my extended critical essay in semester three, I examined the way playwright Tony Kushner constructed the characters of Belize and Roy Cohn to make arguments about racial marginality, political change and democracy in his play *Angels in America*. Writing the paper taught me a number of things about character development and political theatre.

A key feature of the two-year MFA playwriting program at Spalding was the daily workshop that took place for the duration of the residency. At each workshop we read aloud one student's work and discussed its strengths and areas for continued development. It was in these residency workshops that I learned how to give and receive feedback, which is an important skill to develop, and one I have continued to hone since graduation.

8. Is it possible to undertake an arts-based research study as an MA or PhD student?

It is certainly possible to undertake an arts-based research study as an MA or PhD student. However, because such research is generally considered to be "alternative," if not "experimental," arts-based researchers need to find an academic home that supports this kind of work and will provide them with the training and supervision they need to merge social science research and artistic practices. My research into places where graduate students interested in arts-based research practices can find such homes has led me to a number of communities in several American and Canadian universities. This highly selective list is limited to schools located in North America and is based on my personal knowledge of the work undertaken by the academics listed. The list is certainly not exhaustive, and I look forward to learning about other academic homes for graduate students both within and beyond North America. For example, my colleague Catherine Doherty from the Queensland University of Technology (QUT) in Brisbane, Australia, tells me that the creative industries unit at QUT has the capacity to support arts-based research work.

The following list should be seen as a sampling of the academic homes (mostly in my own field of education) that can support an arts-based research study. It is important to remember, however, that these homes are impermanent. Professors retire, move to another university, and find new research interests. It is important to research the current capacity of the departments and universities discussed here to support your arts-based research. You need to make sure that there are enough professors who are available and interested in supervising your arts-based research study before enrolling in any graduate studies program. In creating this list, I have worked with a broad understanding of arts-based research that includes the practices of authoethnography, narrative inquiry, experimental writing, performative writing, as well as the practices of poetry, music, performance, dance, and visual art.

City University of New York (CUNY) Graduate Center

At the CUNY Graduate Center, Michelle Fine's work with youth participatory action research and the Participatory Action Research (PAR) and Design Collective integrates arts-based research practices. The Collective works to examine and document justice and injustice in educational opportunities, sexual and reproductive freedoms, mass incarceration, access to health care and knowledge production. Fine's 2008 book, *Revolutionizing Education: Youth Participatory Action Research in* Motion, edited with Julio Cammarota, provides a sampling of this work.[13]

Ohio State University

At the School of Educational Policy and Leadership at Ohio State University, Patti Lather has written extensively on qualitative research and ethnography after post-structuralism, and teaches courses on qualitative research and feminist methodology. Lather's own engagement with experimental writing appears in the ethnography she wrote with Chris Smithie in 1997 called *Troubling the Angels: Women Living with HIV/AIDS*.[14] She is currently working on a new book called *Engaging (Social) Science: Policy from the Side of the Messy*.

Ontario Institute for Studies in Education, University of Toronto

At the Ontario Institute for Studies in Education, there is a home for graduate students interested in arts-based educational research in the Department of Curriculum, Teaching and Learning. I am interested in performed ethnography and research-informed theatre. Curriculum theorist and sports sociologist Heather Sykes is interested in performed ethnography and performative inquiry, and urban education researcher Kathleen Gallagher has worked with performed ethnography and digital qualitative research. Both Sykes and Gallagher teach graduate courses in post-foundational qualitative research methodology. Curriculum theorist and arts in education researcher Rubén Gaztimbide-Fernandez is interested in the methodology of portraiture, and Stephanie Springgay, curriculum theorist and visual arts researcher, teaches a graduate course called Arts-Based Methodologies. Springgay is also the editor of the *Journal of Curriculum and Pedagogy*, a journal that publishes arts-based research.

Outside the Department of Curriculum Teaching and Learning, Gary Knowles also works with graduate students interested in arts-based research and as mentioned earlier, has co-edited a handbook called *Handbook of the Arts in Qualitative Research: Perspectives, Methodologies, Examples, and Issues*, which was published in 2008.[15]

Simon Fraser University, Canada

Lynn Fels in the Faculty of Education at Simon Fraser University graduated from the University of British Columbia where she worked with several arts-based educational researchers. Fels is interested in performative inquiry and is a member of the editorial team that publishes *Educational Insights*, an on-line journal that is interested in arts-based research.

University of British Columbia, Canada

A group of professors in the Faculty of Education at the University of British Columbia have written an article about their supervision of more than 30 arts-based research dissertations called "Arts-based education research dissertations: Reviewing the practices of new scholars."[16] In the article, Professors Sinner, Leggo, Irwin, Gouzouasis and Grauer identify three major kinds of practices that characterize their students' work: literary, visual and performative.

University of Illinois, Urbana Champagne, USA

At the University of Illinois, Urbana Champagne, Norman Denzin, Research Professor of Communications, has described himself as an ethnographer, an interpretive interactionist, a cultural critic, and an occasional social theorist.[17] Most widely known for the handbooks on qualitative research he co-edits with Yvonna Lincoln, Denzin is also the author of an autoethnography *Searching for Yellowstone: Race, Gender, Family and Memory in the Postmodern West*, published in 2008 and a book called *Performance Ethnography: Critical Pedagogy and the Politics of Culture*, published in 2003.[18] Norman Denzin is also the editor of the journal *Qualitative Inquiry* and the founder of the International Center of Qualitative Research at the University of Illinois, which hosts an annual conference on qualitative research. Both the journal and the conference welcome the submission of arts-based research projects.

University of South Florida, USA

At the University of South Florida, Professor Carolyn Ellis teaches in the Department of Communications. Ellis is interested in emotions, narrative inquiry and autoethnography, and offers graduate courses in autoethnography and communicating emotions. Her recent autoethnographic work includes *Revision: Autoethnographic Reflections on Life and Work* published in 2009 and *The Ethnographic I: A Methodological Novel* published in 2004.[19] Ellis is currently working on a new book called *The Autoethnographic Approach* for Patricia Leavy's Research Series Understanding Qualitative Research.

Also in the Department of Communications Art Bochner teaches a graduate course in narrative inquiry and a writing workshop. His autoethnographic work includes an edited book with Carolyn Ellis called *Ethnographically Speaking: Autoethnography, Literature & Aesthetics* published in 2002.[20] Bochner is also currently working on a new book called *Tales out of School: Meaning and Method in a University Life*.

University of Southern Illinois, Carbondale, USA

In the Department of Speech Communication at the University of Southern Illinois, Carbondale, Ron Pelias is interested in performance studies, performance methodologies and criticism, autoethnography, and performative writing. He has written two recent autoethnographies. The first, *A Methodology of the Heart: Evoking Academic and Daily Life*, was published in 2004, and the second, *Leaning: A Poetics of Personal Relations* was published in 2011.[21]

9. Is there a limit to how much research you can fit into a play? If so, how do you let go of other important research insights?

Like other types research texts, a research-informed play script provides researchers with the space to share some, but not all of their findings. When writing a play, playwrights make decisions about what story or set of stories they will tell in the same way that academics writing an academic article for a social scientific journal make decisions about what they can say about their research findings in the 5,000 words allotted to them. In Chapter One, I referred to writing by American sociologist Yvonna Lincoln, who works with the postmodern idea that all knowledge is partial and historically- and culturally-situated. Lincoln suggests that if all texts are partial, there is only a limited chance that the multiple understandings that come from a research project can be presented in a single text. Knowing that an individual play script can only present some of a study's research findings, playwrights need to be aware of what insights are missing from their play, and must be prepared to create other texts which can present other important insights. In my view it is not a matter of "letting go" of important research findings that do not find their way into a particular play script, but a matter of creating other texts to share research findings that have not been shared yet.

10. Which playwrights have had the most influence on your development as a playwright?

All of the playwrights I have discussed in this book have had an influence on my development as a playwright. The work of other playwrights, theatre artists and academics creating research-based theatre appear in the selected bibliography in Appendix C at the end of the book. While I was studying at Spalding,

I read quite a few interviews with playwrights so I could learn more about their writing process. For my graduation lecture in the fourth semester of my MFA program, I wrote a ten-minute play script that combined excerpts from interviews with American playwrights David Hwang, Tony Kushner, Paula Vogel and August Wilson.[22] Instead of lecturing my classmates and instructors on what these writers had to say, I asked them to read aloud my ten-minute play and then facilitated a discussion of the material included in the play. My audience included both playwrights and screenwriters and I tried to reflect their interests in the script. The play had five scenes:

(1) Writing Plays: Beginning
(2) Writing Plays: Developing a Screenplay from a Play
(3) Writing Plays: Developing a Repertoire of Plays
(4) Staging Plays: The Collaboration Process
(5) Staging Plays: Race, Ethnicity and Culture.

At the end of the play reading and discussion, I provided my classmates and instructors with three questions to take away with them: How do you begin your plays? Do you begin different plays in different ways? How is your own approach similar or different to the playwrights we heard from today? Comparing your own writing process to the process of other writers is a powerful way to learn from them. What have you learned from David Hwang, Tony Kushner, Paula Vogel, and August Wilson? Here are two scene excerpts from my 2006 ten-minute graduation lecture play which I called *In Their Own Words: Hwang, Kushner, Vogel and Wilson on the Process of Writing and Staging Plays*. I chose these two scenes for the way they layer some of the discussions that have been taken up in this book.

Excerpt 1
Writing Plays: Beginning

INTERVIEWER DAVID SAVRAN: How do you usually start a play?

PAULA VOGEL: I usually start by trying to escape, closing myself away from people, going and finding a place that's remote, where I can't be reached. . . . Depending on the play, I spend a little time looking at the ceiling, finding out what my relationship to the material is, where I am. "This is what this play will do for me. Okay, I have to address this, I haven't addressed this yet." I do a lot of reading and research. For example, . . . I did a lot of reading about automobiles for *How I Learned to Drive* . . . I construct a lot of tape loops. I spend a huge amount of money on music . . . [but] I don't have any good music. I have only schlock for a particular play that creates a distinctive sound world. I create a sound loop that I play over and over again . . . Then I do a general plot outline. I try to figure out where I'm going. But I'm not figuring out the absolute ends of my plays anymore. I'm figuring out the beginning points. Then I usually surprise myself in the last moment. Not always, but often. Or the sequence surprises me. You let the plot take over. Take notes, and let her rip. I usually try to get a draft out in two to four weeks . . . I also believe that the best thing to do before I return to rewrites is to start a new play. So I keep an ongoing cycle in which the new play tells me how to change, how to rewrite the older play (Vogel in Savran 1999, 276–277).

INTEVIEWER JACKSON BRYER: When you start writing for the stage, do you start with a visual image?

DAVID HENRY HWANG: I generally start with ideas rather than images, but at different points in my writing career this has gone differently. Right now I generally feel I need to know what the beginning of the play is and what the end of the play is, and the fun of writing them becomes a way to navigate between the two points (Hwang in Bryer 1988, 127).

AUGUST WILSON: I work like this—in collages. I just write stuff down and pile it up, and when I get enough stuff I spread it out and look at and figure out how to use it. You get enough stuff and you start to build the scene and you don't know where the scene's going, and you don't have any idea what's going to follow after that. But once you get the first scene done (or it might be the fourth scene in the play), then you can sort of begin to see other possibilities. Just like working in collages, you shift it around and organize it. This doesn't go here; that speech doesn't really belong to that person, it belongs to this person. So, very much like Romare Bearden (an American collage artist), you move your stuff around on the pages until you have a composition that satisfies you, that expresses the idea of something and then—bingo—you have a play (Wilson in Parks 2005, 25).

INTERVIEWER SUZAN-LORI PARKS: I've never heard anyone say they work like that.

AUGUST WILSON: I didn't know what the hell I was doing [the first time I worked that way], but I remained confident that it would all turn out.

INTERVIEWER SUZAN-LORI PARKS: Where does that confidence come from, man?

AUGUST WILSON: Well . . . I don't know. It comes from an interior life, and as Bearden said, "Art is born out of necessity." So the thing wills itself into being because it has to. Because this is part of your survival, the necessity, the urge to live. It's all part of that together. Confidence is a part of it, and you have to believe that you could dive off a cliff and that you'll be okay, that you'll sprout wings and you'll fly, otherwise you'll never dive off the cliff. So, once you do that the first time, and you do sprout wings, it becomes easier to do that the second time. There's no guarantee, it might be the end of it all. But unless you have confidence, you simply cannot do the work (Wilson in Parks 2005, 25).

Excerpt 2: Staging Plays: The Collaboration Process

INTERVIEWER JACKSON BRYER: From your first production experience through the eight or ten plays you've done, how has that varied? Is it always different?

DAVID HENRY HWANG: I think it's always different . . . Every production experience . . . is a new one. You have to redefine the rules of the engagement as well as the rules of your own part on the collaboration, given the different dynamics that different sets of people represent (Hwang in Bryer 1998, 130).

INTERVIEWER JACKSON BRYER: In this collaborative effort, are there people that you feel closer to than others? What do you get from an actor that's different from, let's say, a director, that's different from a designer?

DAVID HENRY HWANG: The director-playwright relationship is the basic fulcrum on which the production hinges . . . I want to have a certain input with the actors, and I like to deal with them in a rehearsal situation where the actors feel free to comment on the text. I like to hear all the stuff, which is not to say that I'll necessarily go along with it, but I do want to get all the input and see which of it seems to land true. But essentially I think that my [primary] relationship is with the director (Hwang in Bryer 1988, 132).

INTERVIEWER DAVID SAVRAN: How closely do you work with [director] Lloyd Richards [who directed Wilson's plays *Ma Rainey* and *Fences*]?

AUGUST WILSON: Generally I will meet with him an hour before rehearsal and talk about what happened yesterday and what we're going to do today. I don't talk to actors in rehearsal. I talk to Lloyd and he understands and communicates my concerns to the actors. Other than that, I just look at way things are going and I listen. Some things might strike my ear wrong. I might find a certain scene doesn't build the way I thought it did. So I make changes when necessary and come back the next day with new pages.

INTERVIEWER DAVID SAVRAN: What makes a good production of your work?

PAULA VOGEL: A director has to figure out her or his relationship to the material in the way that I did when I started to write the play. So the director says, "This is the tale I want to tell with this script [*Baltimore Waltz*]. Not the relationship of Paula Vogel to her dead brother, but here's the person I'm grieving, or the person I want to celebrate, or here's my homage to my first love affair, or my homage to my brother or sister" (Vogel in Savran 1999, 277).

The two excerpts from my ten-minute play script resonate with several themes that have emerged in this narrative of staging *Harriet's House* and provide me with a good way to end my story. Paula Vogel talks about the importance finding an important topic or issue she wants to address and then reading and researching the topic before beginning to write the first draft of a play. David Hwang starts his plays with an idea he's been thinking about, and August

Wilson uses collage, a technique often used in in arts-based research, to think about the story he wants to tell.

All three playwrights also talk about the importance of collaboration in their work, a theme that is at the heart of this book on writing and producing research-informed theatre. As David Hwang suggests, collaboration in theatre production can be a complicated activity. A playwright needs to define the rules of his or her engagement in a collaborative process with theatre artists and share decision-making with a variety of different people who come to the project with their own personal experiences, social commitments and professional imperatives. At stake is the integrity of the research that informs the project and the authenticity of the stories research participants shared with the playwright. But working through the complexities of collaboration brings its own rewards, for it is the collaboration between a playwright and a team of theatre artists that brings a research-informed theatre project to life.

In choosing the final words to end this story of writing and producing research-informed theatre, I have decided to turn to August Wilson: "Confidence is a part of it, and you have to believe that you could dive off a cliff and that you'll be okay, that you'll sprout wings and you'll fly, otherwise you'll never dive off the cliff." I wish all the aspiring playwrights who read this book the confidence to believe that they can sprout wings as they dive off the cliff. Happy writing.

APPENDIX A

HARRIET'S HOUSE

BY
TARA GOLDSTEIN

Developmental History

An early draft of *Harriet's House* was read and critiqued by Gailey Road Productions' Artistic Director Jocelyn Wickett in the spring of 2009.

A four-day workshop exploring the characters, themes and politics of *Harriet's House* was undertaken by Gailey Road Productions July 13–16, 2009. The workshop was facilitated by Jocelyn Wickett, managed by Gillian Lewis, and archived by Amy Gullage. Collaborating artists were:

Lara Arabian
Clair Acott
Sochi Fried
Jorie Morrow
Sora Olah

The post-workshop draft of the script was read and critiqued by playwrights and actors attending the 2009 International Women's Playwright Conference in Mumbai, India, in November 2009. They were:

Vanessa Adams-Harris (USA)
Kristin Bjorn (Norway)

Hina Siddiqui (India)
Denise Walsh (New Zealand)
Fiona Wheeler (Australia)

Finally, Sharon Singer, writer, poet and facilitator of The Moving Pen writing group, read and critiqued the post-conference draft of the script.

Harriet's House premiered at Hart House Theatre on July 2, 2010, during the Pride Festival in Toronto. Jocelyn Wickett directed the production and music for the production was composed and performed by Dan Parker. The cast featured:

Harriet	Joanne Latimer
Luisa	Supinder Wraich
Ana	Rebecca Applebaum
Anita	Jorie Morrow
Marty	Julie Burris
Clare	Estée Feldman

The production attracted 450 people over its three-day run. *Harriet's House* is the first play of a trilogy of plays about Harriet's family.

Playwright's Notes

(Adapted from the program notes for the 2010 production at Hart House Theatre).

Harriet's House grew out of a series of 10-minute plays I wrote dramatizing moments in the lives of two Toronto families who had adopted children from Colombia.

Each of the 10-minute plays explored a difficult moment in the world of transnational adoptive families and provided a set of characters I could bring to life in a full-length play. I found that play during a trip my partner, Margot, and I took to Provincetown.

Provincetown: Wednesday August 6, 2008

It's the week after Family Week and there are still lots of same-sex families in town. White American parents walk up and down Commercial Street with children who were born in Central America and China. Most parents speak English with their kids but at the public library, in a long line of people waiting to use the bathroom, a mother with a young daughter asks if she can go to the front of the line because "it's an emergency." When we say yes, she speaks to her daughter in Spanish, telling her to hold on, it won't be long. Later that night, Jennie McNulty, a white lesbian comic from Los Angeles, makes a joke during her show: "There are a lot of Asians in Provincetown this week. They're looking for their children." The crowd is surprised. A few people laugh quietly, but most are silent; stunned she'd go there. One man yells out, "Oh, nasty."

The politics of race and language and sexuality are embodied in the mixed-race, same-sex families vacationing in Provincetown and the tensions brought on by these politics are provocative. The story of *Harriet's House* began to percolate. In the spring of 2009, I gave an early draft of the play to Jocelyn Wickett and the following July, Jocelyn facilitated a four-day workshop exploring the characters, themes and politics of *Harriet's House*. During rehearsals, more changes were made to the script as the actors worked with the play. I asked Dan Parker to compose and perform some original music for this production and his wonderful music, which we use to transition from one scene to another can be heard on Dan's website: http://www.myspace.com/dansenseimusic

I expect to continue to develop *Harriet's House* in response to the feedback I receive from its production at Hart House Theatre. If there's something you'd like to ask us about the play, we'd be delighted to hear from you. Write us at: gaileyroad@gmail.com.

Characters

HARRIET: School teacher, mother of three daughters, the first two adopted from Colombia. Jewish. Ages from 44 to 46.

LUISA: Harriet's eldest daughter, adopted from Colombia at the age of 10. Ages from 17 to 19.

ANA: Harriet's middle daughter, adopted from Colombia at the age of 7. Ages from 14 to 16 and is lighter-skinned than Luisa.

CLARE: Harriet's youngest daughter, not adopted. Ages from 11 to 13.

MARTY: School teacher, Harriet's girlfriend/partner. Ages from 39 to 41.

ANITA: Founder of Global Family, an international adoption agency. Harriet's friend. Jewish. Ages from 50–52.

Place

Harriet's kitchen, Toronto, Canada.
An orphanage, Bogotá, Colombia.

Time

The present

Pre-show music

(At the 5-minute call a selection of Dan Parker's music begins. The music fades as the lights come down for scene 1.)

Scene 1 (December)

(HARRIET's kitchen. Dan's Salsa Loop *[Track 2] opens the scene. ANA is in the kitchen dancing to the music. HARRIET and LUISA enter arguing. The music fades.)*

HARRIET: *(Heated)* Over my dead body.

LUISA: Oh, please.

HARRIET: You're going to start university this January, just like we've been planning—

LUISA: *(Calm, cool)* I'm going home.

HARRIET: Colombia's not your home.

ANA: Here we go again.

HARRIET: This is your home.

LUISA: This is *your* home.

HARRIET: You can go in the spring. After classes are done.

LUISA: I'm not waiting.

HARRIET: There's no rush. The Sisters will still need your help at the orphanage in the spring. Or we can all go together in the summer when school finishes.

LUISA: I'm leaving right after New Years.

HARRIET: No you're not.

LUISA: I already bought the ticket.

HARRIET: Then you'll have to cancel it. You're only 17 and you can't go without my permission.

LUISA: I'm going back and you can't stop me.

HARRIET: Yes, I can.

ANA: Just let her go.

HARRIET: I will not!

LUISA: I promised you that I'd finish high school here and I did. I fast-tracked so I could get out early. Now I'm leaving.

HARRIET: What about the scholarship you just won? I assumed that—

LUISA: I don't care about the scholarship.

HARRIET: Don't be crazy. You'll be more useful in Colombia if you go to university. They need doctors, nurses, teach—

LUISA: January 7.

ANA: Just let her go. She might not even like it there. Then she'll come back and go to university. Don't you think?

HARRIET: *(To LUISA)* Will you?

LUISA: I'm going to like it there. It's where I belong.

HARRIET: Maybe, maybe not. You were ten when you left.

LUISA: It's my home. My real home.

HARRIET: How can you say that?

ANA: Do we have to go through this again?

LUISA: You can't take a girl of ten from her home in Colombia and expect her to forget where she comes from.

HARRIET: I never asked you to forget! *(Beat)* I don't want you to go.

LUISA: We've been talking about this for a year. I'm going.

HARRIET: But now you have a scholarship. Give university a chance.

LUISA: No.

HARRIET: One semester. Give it one semester.

LUISA: No.

HARRIET: Why not?

ANA: She wants to find our birth mother.

HARRIET: *(Surprised)* What?

LUISA: Shut up!

ANA: We never found out what happened to her.

HARRIET: She was sick. Very sick. And she couldn't take care of you.

ANA: Maybe she got better. Maybe she's alive.

HARRIET: Is that what you think? You think she's alive?

(Neither LUISA and ANA answer.)

HARRIET: *(Gentle)* If she had gotten better, she would have come back for you. You were at the orphanage for three years and . . .

LUISA: But that doesn't mean she died. Did any of the Sisters ever actually tell you how she died?

HARRIET: *(Thinking)* No, but—

LUISA: I want to know what happened to her. And if she's alive, I want to meet her.

(HARRIET doesn't answer.)

You can understand that, can't you?

(HARRIET doesn't answer.)

Of course you can. You love me. And it's because you love me that you're going to give me permission to go back to Colombia.

HARRIET: When will you come back?

LUISA: When I'm ready.

ANA: Oh, oh.

HARRIET: That's not good enough.

LUISA: *(Defensive)* How do I know when I'll be back when I haven't even gone yet?

HARRIET: You'll come back in August. In time to start university in the fall.

LUISA: I'm not—

HARRIET: If you want my permission to go, you'll come back in August and do a full year of university here. A full year. In exchange for my permission to go now.

ANA: That's fair.

LUISA: Whose side are you on?

ANA: It's a fair deal. You owe her that much. Don't you think?

HARRIET: *(Angry)* No one owes me anything! I am your *mother*! And I'm doing what mothers do! Making sure my daughter gets the best that I can give her. You have a chance to go to university. On scholarship! University is a privilege. How many girls in that orphanage get to go to university? None. That's how many. You get to go. You're going to go. You're going to try it. One year.

ANITA: *(Sticks head into kitchen and returns offstage)* What's taking you so long? People are asking for you.

HARRIET: One year.

(LUISA doesn't answer.)

One year or I don't let you go.

LUISA: All right. One year.

HARRIET: And you'll live at the orphanage with the Sisters like you said you would.

LUISA: Yes.

HARRIET: And you'll call once a week.

LUISA: Yes.

HARRIET: I have your word?

LUISA: Yes.

HARRIET: All right, then.

(HARRIET gives LUISA a kiss.)

ANA: Good. *(ANA takes LUISA's hand)* Let's go dance now. I'm not spending all of Colombia Night in the kitchen arguing.

(As ANA and LUISA leave, ANITA enters peeved.)

ANITA: I'm so mad.

HARRIET: *(Distracted, still upset by what's just happened)* Why?

ANITA: One of the newcomers just asked me: "Isn't it better for the children to be adopted by families living in their birth countries?" If he isn't serious about adopting what's he doing at Colombia Night, wasting my time?

HARRIET: Maybe he *is* serious, but just trying to figure out where he stands on the issue before—

ANITA: *(Angry)* "Issue"? What issue? There's no issue. Children who need a home should get a home. Wherever it is. *(Beat)* Never mind. We need to mingle.

(She starts to leave.)

Aren't you coming?

HARRIET: I need a minute, okay?

(ANITA waves without looking back and leaves. Dan's Salsa Loop *[Track 2] begins again while HARRIET sits down at the island and allows herself to feel the weight of what's she's just done, given LUISA permission to go to Bogotá. The music closes the scene and opens scene 2.)*

Scene 2 (The next day)

(HARRIET's kitchen. HARRIET and her girlfriend MARTY, age 35, are sitting at the island. There are milk and cookies on the island counter.)

MARTY: You're letting her go?

HARRIET: Yeah.

MARTY: What happened?

HARRIET: She used the L word.

MARTY: Lesbian?! You told her about us?

HARRIET: No, no, no. Another L word. Love. She said I'd understand why she had to go back because I loved her.

MARTY: Oh. *(Disappointed)* So you didn't tell her about us.

HARRIET: No.

MARTY: We were going to spend Christmas together.

HARRIET: We *are* going to spend Christmas together.

MARTY: Out of the closet.

HARRIET: I know, I know. But with Luisa leaving in a couple of weeks . . . There's just so much going on right now.

MARTY: There's always a lot going on.

HARRIET: *(Takes her hand)* Don't give up on me.

MARTY: *(Squeezes her hand)* You need to tell them. It's been six months. You've got to trust them. You can't let Luisa go without knowing.

HARRIET: *(Still holding MARTY's hand)* I know, know. It's just that . . . I had no idea how difficult it was going to be. In the beginning, it was all so simple. There were children out there who needed a home. I had a home. There were children who needed a family. I wanted a family. The children were from Colombia. So what? I always thought that when the time came, we'd go back to Colombia together, all four of us. I never imagined that Luisa would insist on going back by herself, that—

(CLARE, age 11, calls out from offstage. HARRIET drops MARTY's hand.)

CLARE: *¡hola*, Harriet!

HARRIET: *¡hola!*

MARTY: She calls you Harriet?

HARRIET: She wants to be just like her sisters. They call me Harriet.

(CLARE enters and gives HARRIET a hug and kiss on both cheeks and takes a cookie.)

How was school?

CLARE: Good. Want to know what I learned in Spanish class? *(Takes a bite of her cookie)* Can I have some milk?

HARRIET: Sure. *(Pours Clare some milk)* Do you remember Marty? You met her that night you came to school with me to help out with the bake sale.

MARTY: Hi.

CLARE: Hi. I learned how to count to fifty. I already knew how to count to forty. Now I can count to fifty. Want to hear?
(Takes a sip of milk).

HARRIET: Where's Ana?

CLARE: Outside. *Cuarenta y uno, cuarenta dos, cuarenta tres* –

HARRIET: What's she doing outside?

CLARE: Talking. *Cuarenta cuatro, cuarenta cinco, cuarenta seis* –

HARRIET: Talking to who?

CLARE: Luisa. *Cuarenta siete,*

HARRIET: Luisa's home too?

CLARE: Yes. *Cuarenta ocho* –

HARRIET: What are they talking about?

CLARE: I'm not sure. They're talking too fast. *Cuarenta neuve, cincuenta!*

MARTY: *Muy bien.*

CLARE: *Graçias.* Wait until Luisa hears!
(LUISA and ANA enter and put their knapsacks down on the floor. There's a lot of after school energy in kitchen, with the girls sometimes talking over each other.)
Want to hear me count from one to fifty? *Uno, dos, tres*—

LUISA: Later. *(To Ana)* Have you seen my blue shirt?

ANA: *(Takes a cookie, pours herself some milk)* No.

LUISA: Are you sure? The last time—

ANA: The last time what?

HARRIET: I just washed it. Say hi to Marty.

LUISA and ANA: *(In unison, like school kids)* Hi Marty.

MARTY: *(Chooses to laugh)* Hi.
(LUISA pours herself some milk.)

CLARE: Is Marty your real name?

MARTY: It's my real name now.

CLARE: What was your real name before?

MARTY: If I tell you, do you promise not to tell anyone else?

CLARE: *(Excited she's getting in on a secret)* Yes.

MARTY: C'mere.
(CLARE goes over to MARTY who leans over and whispers her name into CLARE's ear.)

CLARE: Oh!

ANA: What is it?

CLARE: It's a secret! *(Beat)* Between Marty and me.

LUISA: You want to hear another secret?

CLARE: *(Thrilled)* Yes!

LUISA: I'm going back to Colombia.

CLARE: When?

LUISA: After Christmas.

CLARE: When are you coming back?

HARRIET: *(Quick)* When school starts in the fall.

CLARE: *(Upset)* You're not coming to the cottage this summer with Daddy—I mean Jonathon?

LUISA: No.

CLARE: I don't want you to go.

LUISA: I have to go.

CLARE: Why?

LUISA: I need to find my mother.

CLARE: Harriet's your mother.

HARRIET/LUISA: Her birth mother/My real mother.

CLARE: Harriet's your real mother.

LUISA: She's *your* real mother.

CLARE: *(Reaches out to hug LUISA, but LUISA walks away to get a cookie)* I don't want you to go!

(HARRIET stands up and comforts her.)

HARRIET: Luisa will call once a week. And she'll write to you.

CLARE: *(Hopeful)* In Spanish?

LUISA: *(Laughs)* You don't know how to read Spanish yet.

CLARE: Yes, I do. A little. And Ana can help me. Right?

ANA: *(Reaches for another cookie)* I don't read much better than you.

LUISA: Which is not something to be proud of. So I'll write to both of you in Spanish. So *both* of you can practice.

CLARE: Promise?

LUISA: Promise.

(Dan's Luisa's Ballad-1 *[Track 3] closes the scene and opens scene 3.)*

Scene 3 (January: One month later)

(HARRIET's kitchen. MARTY is helping ANA tape up her hockey stick.)

MARTY: Keep the tape tight. You don't want any bumps.

ANA: Okay.

MARTY: That's good.

ANA: *(Stops taping)* How old were you when you started playing?

MARTY: Older than you. In my twenties. Hardly any girls played hockey when I was in high school.

ANA: Too bad. Don't you think?

MARTY: Yeah.

ANA: Maybe I could come to one of your games sometime.

MARTY: Sure. That'd be great.

ANA: When are they?

MARTY: Monday nights. You could come to one of the early games. They start at 6:30.

ANA: And then maybe you could come to one of mine. We play on Saturdays.

MARTY: How early?

ANA: Not too early. Ten.

MARTY: Ten!

ANA: That's not early!

MARTY: *(Grins)* I know. I was just joking. I'd love to come see you play.

ANA: Have you ever coached?

MARTY: Nope.

ANA: Would you like to?

MARTY: I dunno. I never thought about it. Maybe. Someday.

ANA: *(Starts taping again)* Can I ask you something?

MARTY: What? Be careful, it's a little bumpy there.

ANA: *(Pulls back the tape that made the bump)* Are you and Harriet . . .

MARTY: *(Is silent for a spilt second)* Are me and Harriet what?

ANA: You know . . .

MARTY: Are Harriet and I . . .

ANA: *(Stops taping)* Are you her girlfriend?

(MARTY doesn't answer.)

I don't mean a friend who's a girl. I mean girlfriend.

MARTY: *(Makes a decision)* Yes.

ANA: I knew it!

(ANA walks away and gets a cookie. Her back is to MARTY.)

MARTY: *(Worried)* Is that okay?

ANA: Does Luisa know?

MARTY: I don't know. Harriet was going to tell her before she left, but in the end she didn't. But if you knew, maybe Luisa does too.

ANA: I didn't know until you started coming over. After Luisa left. *(Beat)* Why didn't Harriet tell her?

MARTY: I'm not sure.

ANA: *(Turns to face MARTY)* Luisa can be difficult. Like when we go out shopping to buy clothes? All three of us go to the mall together, and any of the clothes that I like have to be approved by Luisa before we buy them. I actually have two mothers.

MARTY: Really?

ANA: Luisa was the one who took care of me in the orphanage before Harriet and Jonathon adopted us. I was four and she was seven and she took care of me. For three years.

MARTY: Wow.

ANA: Yeah. But just so you know, if you ever decide to live with us, I don't need a third mother.

MARTY: Right.

ANA: Having two is hard enough.

MARTY: Right.

ANA: Do you want to know what I really need?

MARTY: Sure.

ANA: I really need a hockey coach.

MARTY: *(Amused)* Oh, yeah?

ANA: Ours is leaving at the end of the season.

MARTY: That's too bad.

ANA: Yeah. *(Beat)* It's probably a good thing that Harriet didn't tell Luisa. Don't you think?

MARTY: I don't know. It's never good to hide something like this. It comes back to bite you.

ANA: We should tell Harriet that I know.

MARTY: We should. Do you want to tell her or should I?

ANA: I can do it.

MARTY: Okay. What are you going to say?

(HARRIET walks into the living room behind MARTY who doesn't see her come in.)

ANA: *(To HARRIET)* I know about you and Marty. And it's cool.

(MARTY grins.)

HARRIET: You know?!

(MARTY, surprised, turns around quickly to face HARRIET.)

You told her?!

ANA: *(Quick)* I asked her. And it's cool. Marty and I really like each other.

MARTY: *(Grins again)* We do.

ANA: And she's going to be our new hockey coach!

MARTY and HARRIET *(at the same time)*

I am/She is!?

ANA: *(To MARTY)* Yeah. *(Beat)* It'll be fun. Don't you think?

MARTY: *(Grins)* Yeah. It'll be fun. *(To HARRIET)* One down. Two to go.

HARRIET: Three. Three to go. I still need to tell Anita.

ANA: *(To MARTY)* Anita can be nice, but you have to be careful not to get into an argument with her.

HARRIET: Ana!

ANA: I mean I respect her, and everything. She's very devoted to the orphanage. She's always raising money to buy them things they need. Books, clothes, Christmas presents. But, really, you don't want to get her mad.

MARTY: What makes her mad?

ANA: People who say it's better for children to be adopted by families living in their birth countries. She tells them off. *(Speaking in ANITA's voice, passionate, and a little righteous)* Thousands of children who have been abandoned by their families are growing up in orphanages all over the world. Children who need a home should get a home. Wherever it is. Children should never be the victims of politics. *(Speaking in her own voice)* So be careful when you meet her. Don't get into an argument.

HARRIET: *(To MARTY)* What you have to understand is that Anita is adopted herself. And because she's—

ANA: I'm going outside and try out my stick.

HARRIET: Oh. Okay. *(Beat)* So everything's okay?

ANA: *(Kisses HARRIET on the cheek)* Yes. Everything's okay. Don't worry.

(ANA leaves with her hockey stick.)

MARTY: *(Anxious)* Are you mad? It just came out. I didn't plan to tell her or anything. She just asked. Out of the blue. And I don't like lying. Especially about being gay. I never lie about being gay. So I told her. I know it wasn't my place but –

HARRIET: *(Puts her arms around her)* It's fine. Don't worry. You heard her. It's okay. Everything's okay.

MARTY: As long as I don't get into an argument with Anita.

(They laugh. They hug. They laugh).

We're out! We're finally out. It feels great, doesn't it?

HARRIET: *(Steps out of the hug and looks at* MARTY*)* Yeah. It does. It really does. It feels great.

(She takes MARTY*'s hand and gives her a kiss. A lover's kiss.)*

(Dan's Uncertainty *[Track 4] closes the scene and opens scene 4.)*

Scene 4 (March: Two months later)

(HARRIET'S kitchen. HARRIET and ANITA are making sandwiches. There is a jar of mustard, the fixings for sandwiches and a dishtowel.)

ANITA: I know it's last minute, but Belinda—

HARRIET: Cancelled at the last minute. No problem. I'm happy to do it.

ANITA: You're a doll. You always come through for me. You know what newcomers want to know. They want to know what—

HARRIET: Adopting Luisa and Ana was like.

ANITA: And how long—

HARRIET: We had to wait.

ANITA: If you had any—

HARRIET: Problems in Colombia. *(Laughs)* Don't worry, I know.

ANITA: *(Warm)* Of course you know. So you'll come next Sunday. Seven to—

HARRIET: Nine. I'll be there.

ANITA: *(Warm)* Thank you.

HARRIET: You're welcome. How many of these do we need to make?

ANITA: Twenty. Can you keep them in your fridge for now? I'll pick them up later.

HARRIET: Sure. I'll make room. Somehow.

ANITA: It's so busy this time of year. There's the annual advisory board meeting tonight and Passover is just around the corner. You and the girls are able to come?

HARRIET: *(Excited, waiting for the invitation)* We'd love to come. *(Beat, takes a nervous breath)* How do you feel about me bringing a friend?

ANITA: *(Teases)* A special friend?

HARRIET: Yeah.

ANITA: Finally! *Mazel Tov!* Do you have enough Saran to cover the sandwiches?

HARRIET: I think so.

ANITA: Good. So what's his name?

HARRIET: *(Soft)* It's not a him.

ANITA: Sorry, what?

HARRIET: *(Too loud)* It's not a him. It's a her.

ANITA: *(Not sure she's heard right)* What?

HARRIET: I'm seeing a woman.

ANITA: You're seeing a woman?

HARRIET: Yes. I know it's a bit of a surprise.

ANITA: I'll say.

HARRIET: It was a surprise for me too. *(Pause)* Okay. So you're happy for me, right?

ANITA: Do the girls know?

HARRIET: Ana and Clare know. And they both really like Marty.

ANITA: Marty?

HARRIET: It's a nickname. For Martha.

(ANITA doesn't answer.)

You're upset.

ANITA: Of course, I'm upset. This changes everything.

HARRIET: How? I'm still me.

ANITA: *(Intense)* No, you're not. My Harriet was married for 13 years. I always assumed you'd get married again. Now all of a sudden you're, you're . . .

HARRIET: *(Light)* Coming out!

ANITA: *(Remembers the phrase)* Coming out of the cupboard!

HARRIET: *(Hides a smile)* Closet.

ANITA: What?

HARRIET: People say they're coming out of the closet.

ANITA: Whatever. How long have you known? That you're a, a . . .

HARRIET: Lesbian? A while.

ANITA: And you never thought to mention it?

HARRIET: I guess I was afraid.

ANITA: Of what?

HARRIET: Of this! *(Beat)* Look, when Marty comes to Seder, you'll have a chance to get to know her and once you do –

ANITA: Seder's for family. We need to finish up here. It's getting late.

HARRIET: I'm family. Ana and Clare are family.

ANITA: You and Ana and Clare can come.

HARRIET: What if I won't come unless Marty comes too?

ANITA: Then you won't come.

HARRIET: If I don't come, then Ana and Clare won't come.

(ANITA doesn't answer.)

Clare's been practicing the four questions for weeks. In Spanish as well as Hebrew and English. You can't disappoint her.

ANITA: I'm not the one who's going to disappoint her. *(Points her mustard covered knife at HARRIET)* You are.

(She gets mustard on her blouse.)

Shit!

(She grabs the dishtowel and tries to take the mustard off her blouse.)
Shit, shit, shit.
(She looks at her blouse.)
I need to wash this off before it stains.
(ANITA begins to leave, dishtowel in hand.)

HARRIET: *(Calls after her)* But I've already invited her.
(ANITA stops.)

ANITA: Well you shouldn't have.

HARRIET: Why?

ANITA: You're not the only one who comes to Global Seder. I have the other families to think about. Not everyone will approve of your new lifestyle, you know.

HARRIET: But we're the only Globals who are actually Jewish. You and I and the girls, we've been doing Seder from the very beginning.

ANITA: You think I don't know that?

HARRIET: Look, Anita. You're the force behind Global Family. You set the tone. If you make Marty welcome, so will they.

ANITA: *(Scrubs at the mustard stain on her blouse, then)* The others won't approve. They'll call me up the next day and tell me that the girls should be living in a family with a mother and a father. They'll say Ana and Clare's lives are complicated enough without having kids at school calling them names because their mother is a . . . a . . .

HARRIET: *(Getting heated)* Lesbian, Anita. The word is lesbian. Look, they'll learn to deal with the homophobia the same way they learned to deal with the racism. What will make their lives more complicated is if you abandon us.

ANITA: *(Scrubs at the stain again)* Who's abandoning you? You and the girls can all come to Seder.

HARRIET: But only if we come without Marty.

ANITA: Look, you don't know how serious this is. What if it's just a fling?

HARRIET: *(More heated)* It's not a fling. *(Beat)* Not all gay relationships are casual, you know.

ANITA: If you're still together a year from now, then we'll talk.

HARRIET: You didn't make Belinda wait a year before you invited the new man in her life to come to Seder.

ANITA: That was different.

HARRIET: How?

ANITA: I had a chance to get to know him. He was becoming part of the family.

HARRIET: If you invite Marty to Seder, you'll get to know her too.

ANITA: Seder's not the place to get to know someone.

HARRIET: All right. Come over for dinner then. Before Seder. Pick a night. Any night.

ANITA: I can't. Not before Seder. Maybe after.

HARRIET: *(Angry)* This is so ironic. Seder is all about escaping and fighting oppression and here you are oppressing me and Marty because you're afraid of what other people might think!

ANITA: *(Angry)* Hey! First of all, I don't need a lecture from you about the meaning of Seder. And second of all, it's not just about you and Marty. There are laws against gay people adopting children in lots of countries. What's legal here is not legal everywhere. I have the reputation of my agency to think about. All those kids waiting to be adopted are depending up me. *(Looks at her blouse)* I'm going home to put on a new blouse. This one's ruined. Call me if you change your mind. *(Beat)* I'll send someone over to pick up the sandwiches. *(ANITA leaves. HARRIET is devastated. Her cheeks are hot with anger. She begins to make another sandwich and then stops and slams the knife on the counter.)*

Scene 5 (August: Five months later)

(HARRIET's kitchen. Dan's Pop Song [Track 5] opens the scene. There's a "Welcome Home Luisa" sign that Clare made that is attached to the island. HARRIET and CLARE wait for LUISA to wake up and come into the kitchen. HARRIET skims through the newspaper as she waits. The music fades.)

CLARE: It's almost time for lunch. Can't I wake her up?

HARRIET: No. Let her sleep.

CLARE: Why didn't you wake me up when you got home?

HARRIET: It was one in the morning.

CLARE: So?

HARRIET: She was tired. She wanted to go straight to bed.

CLARE: How does she look?

HARRIET: Good. But tired.

CLARE: Is she glad to be back?

HARRIET: *(Hesitates)* Of course.

CLARE: I can't wait. I'm going to wake her up.

HARRIET: *(Quick)* No. Don't.

(LUISA enters in her pajamas.)

LUISA: It's okay. I'm up.

(CLARE runs over to her and throws her arms around her waist.)

CLARE: Luisa! You're home! You're finally home!

LUISA: Just like I promised.

CLARE: Did you see my welcome home sign?

LUISA: No! Where is it?

CLARE: *(She points to the sign)* Right here!

LUISA: Let me take a look at it.

(She takes a long look at the sign)

Que bella.

(She kisses CLARE on both cheeks.)

Gracias, Clara.

(CLARE is thrilled.)

I bought some presents for you and Ana and Harriet. They're up in my room in a big red cloth bag. Go find them.

CLARE: Okay. I'll be back in a minute.
(She leaves.)
HARRIET: How did you sleep?
LUISA: Okay.
HARRIET: Are you hungry?
LUISA: No. I woke up at 6:00 so I made a grilled cheese sandwich and went back to bed.
HARRIET: It's wonderful to have you back.
LUISA: *(Smiles)* It's nice to be back. *(Beat)* I meant what I said last night. I'll stay and visit for a few weeks, but then I'm going back.
HARRIET: We'll talk about it later, once you've had a chance to settle in.
LUISA: I'm not going to change my mind. I can't focus on school or anything else until I find out what happened to her.
HARRIET: No one can tell you anything?
LUISA: If the Sisters know anything, they're not saying.
HARRIET: Why?
LUISA: Who knows? Maybe because she asked them not to. But the longer I work there, the more they'll trust me, and if I keep on asking one day someone will tell me.
HARRIET: Do you really think so?
LUISA: Yes. *(Beat)* So what's new around here?
HARRIET: Well, actually, there *is* something important that's happened just before you left –
CLARE: *(Enters with the red bag)* I'm back!
LUISA: *(Laughs)* That was fast! Bring it over and I'll show you what I've brought!
(HARRIET swallows her disappointment at missing her opportunity to tell LUISA about MARTY so that the moment won't be ruined for CLARE.)
(As LUISA hands out her gifts to CLARE and HARRIET Dan's Pop Song *[Track 5] closes the scene and opens scene 6.)*

Scene 6 (That night)

(HARRIET's kitchen. ANA and LUISA are at the island drying dishes, pots and pans. The music fades.)
LUISA: *Estas cambiada.* ("You're different," in a fundamental way.)
ANA: You think?
LUISA: *Y no para bien* ("And not in a good way.")
(ANA shrugs her shoulders.)
Ya no hablas español. ("You don't speak Spanish anymore.")
ANA: So what?
LUISA: *Es nuestro idioma.* ("It's our language.")
ANA: Speak Spanish with Clare. She can count up to a thousand now.
LUISA: *¡ Caramba muchacha!* ["Jesus, girl!"] *No quiero hablar español con Clare. Yo quiero hablar contigo.* ("I don't want to speak Spanish with Clare. I want to speak Spanish with you.")

(ANA shrugs her shoulders.)

Quiero que no lo tierdas. ("I don't want you to lose it.")

ANA: You've been home for less than twenty-four hours and already you're bossing me around. I don't need it here.

LUISA: *Aquí no vas a pasar toda la vida.* ("You're not going to be here all your life.")

ANA: *(Grounded)* Yes, I am.

LUISA: *(Switches to English)* No, you aren't. You're going to go back someday.

ANA: How do you know?

LUISA: You're going to be curious.

ANA: About what?

LUISA: About how people in Colombia live. What our culture's like, what our music's like.

ANA: *(Puts down the dish/pot she's dried)* I know what Colombian music's like. I've heard it. Lots of times.

(She takes her dishtowel and snaps it against LUISAS's backside playfully. It doesn't hurt.)

LUISA: Ow!

(She takes her dishtowel and tries to snap it against ANA's backside, but ANA moves away too quickly. Ana laughs.)

There's more to Colombian music than Shakira, you know.

ANA: *(Picks up another pot, still grounded)* I like Shakira.

LUISA: *(Excited)* You need to hear some Reggaetón.

ANA: Shakira sings Reggaetón.

(She begins to sing Hips Don't Lie from Shakira's Oral Fixation *CD.)*

LUISA: I mean real Reggaetón. *(Puts down the pot she's dried)* I want you to come back with me next summer.

ANA: I already have plans.

LUISA: What plans?

ANA: *(Puts down the pot she's dried and picks up a third one)* I'm going to work at Brian's camp.

LUISA: Brian, Brian, Brian. All I hear about is Brian. *(Beat)* He's the reason you don't speak Spanish anymore. He's the reason you act white.

ANA: You're behind, I've done four you've done one.

LUISA: *(Picks up a pan/dish)* Three. You've done three. *(Beat)* Don't you want to meet her?

ANA: Who?

LUISA: Our Mamá.

ANA: *(Puts down the dried pot and picks up another one and waves it in LUISA's face)* I'm way ahead of you. We should get the dishes done before Harriet gets back. Are you going to help?

LUISA: Where is she?

ANA: She's at the doctor. She told you.

LUISA: *(Starts drying again)* We have to find out what happened to her.

ANA: Harriet?

LUISA: No. Our Mamá.

ANA: If you haven't found out by now, she's probably dead.

LUISA: But there's no record of her death in our files. The Sisters looked.

ANA: So?

LUISA: So, there's a chance that she's still alive. And that one day I'll find her and we'll get a chance to meet her.

ANA: I don't need to meet her.

LUISA: I don't believe you. *(Puts down the pot.)* Maybe you look like her.

ANA: *(Suddenly angry)* Even if I do look like her, I'd never act like her. Every single thing inside of me comes from living here. In this family. In this country. *(Raises her voice)* If you want to go back to Colombia, go! You want to look for a woman who left us and who is probably dead, go! Go look for her. But I'm staying here.

(HARRIET enters.)

HARRIET: What's going on?

LUISA: Nothing.

HARRIET: *(To ANA)* Why are you shouting?

ANA: She made me mad.

HARRIET: *(Light)* Just like old times.

LUISA: All I did was ask her to come to Colombia with me next summer and she freaked out.

ANA: I didn't freak out.

LUISA: Yes, you did.

(Puts down the pot she's drying, picks up another one.)

ANA: *(Angry)* No, I didn't. I told you that I'm not going because I've got other plans. You just can't take no for an answer.

HARRIET: *(To ANA)* You don't want to go?

ANA: *(Trying to be calm)* No.

HARRIET: *(Trying to buffer the tension)* Well, there's no rush. Most of the other Global kids don't go back until they finish high school. You have plenty of time.

LUISA: *(Exasperated, puts the pot down with a bang)* You shouldn't try and influence her that way.

HARRIET: I wasn't trying to influence her. I just said there's no rush.

LUISA: Yes, there is a rush. She's not speaking Spanish anymore. She's losing it. *(Accusatory)* She's being robbed of our heritage.

HARRIET: And that's my fault?!

(CLARE, who has been standing in the doorway quietly enters.)

LUISA: She doesn't have a chance to practice. She spends all her time with Brian. She doesn't see any of the Globals anymore. Clare says you didn't go to Seder and you haven't been to any of the events since Passover. What's that about?

HARRIET: *(Worried now)* That's a long story . . . Let me make some tea and we can –

CLARE: I can do it.

HARRIET: No, that's okay. Honey. I'll do it.

LUISA: What happened?

ANA: It's because of Marty.

LUISA: Marty? Who's Marty?

HARRIET: You remember my friend Marty. From school?

ANA: She's my new hockey coach.

CLARE: And she's Harriet's –

HARRIET: Clare, honey, could you go next door and ask to borrow some milk for the tea? We're all out.

CLARE: Okay. Luisa, do you want to come with me?

LUISA: No.You go. I'll stay here.

CLARE: Okay. *¡hasta luego!*

(CLARE leaves.)

LUISA: So what's the problem with Marty? Anita doesn't like her?

HARRIET: Anita has never even met her.

LUISA: So then why – ?

HARRIET: Marty's gay.

LUISA: So?

HARRIET: *(Brave, defiant)* And so am I. She's my partner now and Anita doesn't approve.

(There's a second or two of silence while Luisa absorbs the news.)

LUISA: She's your partner?

(HARRIET nods.)

You're with a woman?

(HARRIET nods.)

Why didn't you tell me? I called every Sunday. You could have said something!

HARRIET: I wanted to . . . but you were so full of stories of what you were doing in Colombia . . . they seemed more interesting than my . . . I don't know. I should've told you. I'm sorry.

LUISA: Sorry's not good enough.

HARRIET: Sorry's what I have to offer.

ANA: There's nothing to be sorry about. Marty's great. Everyone likes her. I like her, Clare likes her. She's even got Clare coming to our games.

LUISA: Are you planning on moving in together?

HARRIET: Someday.

LUISA: Someday soon?

HARRIET: I don't know. Maybe.

LUISA: With Ana and Clare still living here?

HARRIET: Maybe. Why not?

ANA: Marty's great!

LUISA: Sshh.

ANA: Don't sshh me! This isn't Colombia. I'm not one of your orphans who you can sshh.

LUISA: *(Ignores ANA, to HARRIET)* I don't think she should move in here.

HARRIET: Well, it's not your decision to make.

LUISA: Fine. I'm not staying anyway.

HARRIET: You made a promise that you'd go back to school if I let you go to Bogotá. You promised to give it a year. All your registration material is sitting here, waiting for you. I want you back to school next week. Just like you promised.

LUISA: I don't care about what you want or don't want. I'm done listening to you. I'm done hearing what you want me to do and not do. I'm eighteen now and I am going to do what I *want*. I'm not interested in going back to school. There's only one thing I'm interested in. Finding out what happened to my real mother.

(LUISA leaves. ANA and HARRIET look at each other in dismay and then ANA goes over to give HARRIET a hug.)

HARRIET: What am I going to do about your sister?

ANA: What can you do? You have to let her go.

(Dan's Luisa's Ballad-2 *[Track 6] closes the scene and opens scene 7.)*

Scene 7 (September: One month later)

(HARRIET's kitchen. MARTY is moving into HARRIET's house. She, ANA and CLARE are unpacking some of her boxes.)

ANA: Look at this!

(She unrolls a set of silver candlesticks from the white tissue paper they've been wrapped in.)

MARTY: Be careful with those. They belonged to my grandmother. She used to light them on Rosh Hashana and Passover.

CLARE: How many people did she invite?

MARTY: Thirty.

CLARE: Thirty! Anita only invites fifteen because that's already a lot of work. But this year she only had twelve because we didn't go.

ANA: No one cares.

CLARE: I care. I was supposed to say the four questions in Spanish.

ANA: Ancient history. *(To MARTY)* Tell us more about your grandmother. Did she live in a big house?

MARTY: No. In a small one-bedroom apartment.

ANA: So how could she invite thirty people?

MARTY: She borrowed four small bridge tables and thirty fold-up chairs.

CLARE: From who?

MARTY: The relatives and neighbours. I used to help her. After that she covered the tables with a white linen tablecloth that her mother, my great grandmother, had embroidered by hand. With blue and gold thread. For the holidays, she'd take out her white and gold china and crystal glasses and put some flowers in the middle. Her kitchen was tiny. There was only room for one person to work in there. But somehow she managed to feed thirty people a seven-course meal. I don't know she did it.

ANA: She sounds amazing. You must have really loved her.

MARTY: I did. She was the most generous person I've ever known. Your mum is like her.

CLARE: Is she still alive?

MARTY: No.

CLARE: How did she die?

MARTY: *(Lowers her eyes)* She had cancer.

ANA: What kind of cancer?

MARTY: *(Looks up at ANA)* Breast cancer.

CLARE: *(Anxious)* Like Harriet?

ANA: Shut up!

MARTY: Hey, we don't know for sure if your mum has cancer. All we know is that she has a lump on her breast. That's why they did the test they did today. To find out. Maybe she has cancer, but we're hoping she doesn't.

ANA: I don't want to talk about it.

MARTY: Okay. Why don't you open another box?

CLARE: *(Panicked)* If Harriet has cancer is she going to die? Like your grandmother?

ANA: *(Loud)* Shut up! Shut up! Shut up!

MARTY: *(A little sharp)* Sshh. Lower your voice. Your mum's trying to sleep.

ANA: You can't tell me to shut up. You're not my mother.

MARTY: I didn't tell you to shut up. I told you to lower your voice. You're the one who told Clare to shut up.

CLARE: Yeah!

ANA: Why don't you just go home? And take your grandmother's ugly old candlesticks with you!

(She throws the candlesticks into the box she was emptying.)

MARTY: *(Surprised)* Ana! Be careful. *(Raises her voice)* Watch what you're doing!

ANA: Don't yell at me!

MARTY: *(Tries to calm down)* I'm not yelling. I'm just telling you to be careful.

(CLARE starts sniffing. MARTY goes over to CLARE and sits her in her lap.)

ANA: I want you to go back to your place.

CLARE: No!

ANA: When Harriet wakes up I'm going to tell her that we don't want you here.

CLARE: No!

MARTY: *(To CLARE)* Don't worry honey. I'm not going anywhere. *(To ANA)* Kicking me out isn't going to make that lump on her breast go away.

ANA: What!

MARTY: You heard me.

(ANA is silent for a few seconds. Then she stalks off stage.)

Shit. *(Calls out with CLARE still in her lap)* Ana, come back. I'm sorry. I'm sorry I raised my voice. I was upset. Come back. Come back and we'll finish unpacking. Then we'll go for some ice cream. Okay?

(ANA doesn't respond.)

MARTY: Shit.

CLARE: You said "shit"! Twice.

MARTY: I know. Don't tell anyone, okay?

CLARE: Okay. I won't.

MARTY: Do you want to help me unpack the rest of my stuff? There's not much left.

CLARE: Then can we go for ice cream? Even if Ana doesn't come?

MARTY: Sure. We deserve a treat after all this work.

(They begin to unpack the boxes again. ANA enters and goes over to the box with the candlesticks. She picks them up carefully and puts them on the island. Lights fade.)

(Dan's Cancer *[Track 7] closes the scene and opens scene 8.)*

Scene 8 (March: Six months later)

(HARRIET's kitchen. HARRIET and MARTY are coming in from a walk and taking off their winter jackets, hats and gloves. Under her winter hat HARRIET is wearing a bandana that covers her bald head.)

MARTY: They're not going to want to go. Not if you're not well.

HARRIET: *(Determined)* I'll be fine.

MARTY: We should wait until you're healthy again.

HARRIET: Ana needs to go back now.

MARTY: But she doesn't want to go back.

HARRIET: It doesn't matter. Luisa's been gone for seven months. A year and a half altogether. It's time to go visit her.

MARTY: What about us? You and me? How will that play out?

HARRIET: No one there has to know about us.

MARTY: *(Sharp)* What?

HARRIET: It'll make things easier.

MARTY: For whom? Look, either we're a family or we're not. *(Hurt)* I thought I was part of your family.

HARRIET: *(Quick)* Of course you're part of the family. *(Goes over to hug her)* I'm crazy about you, the girls adore you, and I don't know how we would have made it through chemo without you! But we can't be out as a family in Colombia. People won't understand.

MARTY: That's their problem.

HARRIET: And ours. We can't visit Luisa at the orphanage without the Sisters' permission. They might not give it to us if they know.

MARTY: So what do you want? For me to pose as Ana and Clare's "Aunt"? A family friend?

HARRIET: *(Sits down on the stool behind the island)* If that's what it takes.

MARTY: *(Emphatic)* I hate pretending.

HARRIET: I know. What choice do we have?

(Pause. MARTY walks over to the window.)

MARTY: They've taken the boards of the hockey rink down. Hockey's officially over for the season.

HARRIET: How many afternoons and nights did you spend out there this winter?

MARTY: Lots.

HARRIET: Lacing up skates. Taping up sticks. *(Beat)* I'm really sorry Ana didn't play in the playoffs.

MARTY: She wanted to be with you during your last round of chemo. She'll play again next year.

HARRIET: And you'll coach her team again?

MARTY: Only if you promise to bring us some of your famous hot chocolate.

HARRIET: I promise.

MARTY: Are you sure, really sure, you're well enough to travel?

HARRIET: *(Determined)* I'm sure.

MARTY: *(Starts pacing, upset)* We don't even know if the chemo worked!

HARRIET: It doesn't matter. All that matters is that right now I'm strong enough to go.

MARTY: Are you sure that Luisa will see us?

HARRIET: She'll see us.

MARTY: How do you know?

HARRIET: She's called every week since I started chemo. She's upset. And living far away. She needs to connect. With all of us. You too. I think I need to lie down for a bit.

MARTY: *(Takes her arm and helps her get off the stool)* Let me help you. We shouldn't have gone out for so long.

HARRIET: Don't worry. I'm fine.

MARTY: No, you're not.

HARRIET: I'm fine enough.

MARTY: *(Upset)* And what if you don't stay fine enough? What if I end up losing you and the girls go and live with their father? What if I lose all three of you at once?

(HARRIET moves and gives MARTY a hug.)

HARRIET: I love you. And so do they. Everything's going to be okay. *(Carefully breaks out of the hug)* But I need to take the girls to Colombia. So I'll have no regrets.

MARTY: *(Looks at her for a second or two)* Everyone has regrets.

HARRIET: So I won't have that regret.

(Dan's Reggaetón *[Track 8] closes the scene and opens scene 9.)*

Scene 9 (April: One month later)

(Outside an orphanage in Bogotá. Morning. HARRIET, MARTY, ANA, [now age 16] and CLARE [now age 12] are sitting on two benches, waiting for LUISA to arrive. There are several bottles of water beside each bench. HARRIET is still wearing a bandana over her bald head. The music fades).

CLARE: What's taking her so long?

HARRIET: The Sisters went to tell her we're here. She'll come out soon.

CLARE: I can't wait to see her!

(LUISA, now age 19, enters. She's very thin and very sad. CLARE runs to greet her. The others stand up.)

CLARE: *(Joyous)* ¡hola, Luisa! Como estas?

(CLARE throws her arms around LUISA'S waist)

You're so thin.

(She stands back to take a look at her face and takes Luisa's hands in her own. LUISA stares at HARRIET and the bandana. It's devastating.)

(HARRIET walks over to CLARE and LUISA. ANA and MARTY hang back.)

LUISA: *(Soft)* hola, Harriet.

HARRIET: I'm very, very glad to see you.

LUISA: *(Hugs HARRIET carefully and touches her bandana)* Welcome back to Colombia. I've missed you.

HARRIET: *(Hugs her back)* I missed you too.

LUISA: *(Looks over to ANA)* Hola, Ana! Aren't you going to say hello?

ANA: *(Doesn't move)* Hi. This is Marty.

LUISA: *(To MARTY)* I remember. *(Beat)*. Thank you for coming.

MARTY: I'm glad to be here.

CLARE: Me too. I'm glad to be here too. I couldn't wait to see you! *(Throws her arms around LUISA's waist and holds on)* You're so thin!

LUISA: *(Looks at ANA)* I found out what happened to Inés.

CLARE: Your birth mother?

(MARTY puts her arm around ANA's shoulders.)

LUISA: She's dead.

HARRIET: *(Reaches out and takes LUISA's hand)* Honey, I'm sorry. I'm so, so sorry.

LUISA: *(Squeezes HARRIET'S hand)* She died right after she left us at the orphanage. She was sick and she died.

(LUISA breaks away from CLARE's hug and walks over to ANA who has begun to cry.)

Our Mamá's dead.

(ANA continues crying. MARTY holds her tighter. HARRIET begins to sway. CLARE grabs a hold of her.)

MARTY: Clare, help Harriet back to the bench so she can sit down.

(CLARE helps HARRIET back to the bench. MARTY opens a bottle of water for HARRIET. HARRIET takes the bottle from MARTY and sits down. CLARE stands beside her.)

CLARE: How did you find out?

LUISA: Sister Francesca told me. She wanted to tell me before, but the other Sisters told her not to.

ANA: How did she die?

LUISA: She had pneumonia. Do you remember her coughing?

(ANA shakes her head.)

I do. I remember her coughing.

CLARE: Why didn't she go to the walk-in clinic and get antibiotics?

LUISA: There was no walk-in clinic. There were no antibiotics. The people here are very, very poor. You can't imagine how poor they are. She got pneumonia and she died. She wasn't strong enough to survive.

HARRIET: *(Soft)* But she was strong enough to make sure that her daughters would survive. She was strong enough to take them to a place where they would be cared for. She was strong enough to make sure that you and Ana would live even if she didn't. *(In tears)* Imagine the strength she had to have had to do that. *(Beat)* You have her strength. You have your mother's strength.

(LUISA doesn't respond, but she is grateful. CLARE, very upset, gets up, walks over to LUISA and puts her arms around her waist again.)

CLARE: I'm sorry. I'm sorry your mother died.

(LUISA puts her hand on CLARE's head.)

LUISA: Me too. I wanted to see her again. Talk to her again. *(To ANA)* Now we never will.

ANA: At least we know what happened to her. You found out. Now we can move on.

LUISA: *(In disbelief)* Move on? I came back to find our *mamá* and get back the years I lost with her. There's nothing to move on to.

(There's an awkward silence for several seconds.)

HARRIET: *(Gentle)* Maybe it seems that way right now, but –

LUISA: Never mind. It doesn't matter. Let's go in. The Sisters are waiting for us.

ANA: I don't want to go in.

LUISA: You have to go in. They're waiting to see you.

ANA: I don't care.

LUISA: *(Stares at ANA)* How can you be so selfish! They were the ones who took care of us when no else did. It won't kill you to visit.

ANA: *(To HARRIET)* You told me that if I didn't want to go inside the orphanage I didn't have to.

LUISA: *(Still staring at ANA)* What's wrong with you?

CLARE: Maybe she's afraid.

LUISA: *(Still staring at ANA)* Of what?

CLARE: Of being sad. Even sadder than we already are.

(ANA bursts into tears.)

HARRIET: *(Gentle)* Look, the news about your mother . . . It's a shock. She needs some time. Maybe tomorrow. We'll all come visit the Sisters tomorrow. But take Clare inside with you now. She has something to give you and the Sisters. *(To CLARE)* Tell her what you've brought with you.

CLARE: It's a cheque.

LUISA: *(Surprised)* What?

CLARE: For $10,000. Canadian. We raised it at my school. Lots of the teachers at my school remember you and Ana. They remember when you first arrived from Colombia. They said they never met a child as brave and capable as you. They wanted to help you. In your work at the orphanage.

LUISA: $10,000 is a lot of money.

(CLARE walks over and takes LUISA's hand.)

CLARE: Maybe we could begin another campaign. A bigger one. To raise money for a clinic.

HARRIET: And you could come back and stay with us. *(Quick)* Just for a while. To kick-start the campaign.

CLARE: *(Puts her arms around LUISA's waist)* You can speak at my school. And Ana's school. And all the other schools in Toronto!

(LUISA looks at ANA who says nothing.)

HARRIET: *(Soft)* We'll all help out. *(Beat)* Your sisters need you now. Come back with us. *(Slight pause)* Please.

(Dan's Luisa's Ballad *[Track 9] closes the scene and opens scene 10.)*

Scene 10 (The Next Day)

(Outside an orphanage in Bogotá. Afternoon. LUISA and ANA are sitting on a bench.)

ANA: Everything is so much smaller.

LUISA: Yeah. I thought so too when I first got here.

ANA: The blackboard was bigger. The window.

LUISA: The bookshelf near the door.

ANA: It's really hot here.

LUISA: You get used to it.

ANA: It's hard to breathe.

LUISA: Take slower breaths.

(ANA slows down her breathing.)

And drink some water. That will help.

(ANA drinks some water.)

I'm glad you're here.

(ANA drinks some more water.)

ANA: I feel like I might pass out.

LUISA: You're probably dehydrated. Keep drinking. But sip it slowly.

(ANA sips some more water.)

So did you remember any of the Sisters?

ANA: *(Soft)* All of them.

(She sips some more water.)

LUISA: Me too. I remembered all of them. It's incredible what they've done here with so little money.

(ANA sips some more water.)

ANA: Everyone here's so poor.

LUISA: I know.

ANA: Do you ever think about what would have happened if we had stayed here?

LUISA: Yes.

ANA: We would've had nothing.

LUISA: We'd be out working.

ANA: Doing what?

LUISA: I don't know. A few of the girls work in the orphanage. Cooking meals, doing laundry. Because I finished high school and can speak and write in English, I'm allowed to teach. Lots of the girls go out and clean people's houses.

ANA: I'd hate that.

LUISA: It's safer than working in the sex trade. Lots of poor girls do that.

(ANA is shocked and is silent for a few seconds.)

ANA: Do you ever feel guilty?

LUISA: That we got to leave?

ANA: *(Takes a sip of water)* Yeah.

LUISA: No. What I feel is mad. Our *mamá* didn't have to die. People don't have to die of pneumonia. If she hadn't been so poor she would've seen a doctor and gotten antibiotics. And she wouldn't have had to leave her two little girls in an orphanage to be adopted by a family who lived a world away from everything they knew and loved.

ANA: I feel guilty.

LUISA: Feeling guilty doesn't help anyone. Or change anything. I want to change things.

ANA: How?

LUISA: I don't know yet.

ANA: Are you coming back with us?

LUISA: Maybe.

ANA: Whose room would you sleep in?

(She drinks some water.)

LUISA: I don't know. My old room I guess.

ANA: You mean *our* old room. Which is my room now.

LUISA: *(Hurt)* You want me to share with Clare?

ANA: That depends.

LUISA: On what?

ANA: *(Takes another sip of water)* If you're coming back as my sister or my mother.

LUISA: What's that supposed to mean?

ANA: It means I don't want to have two mothers again. You and Harriet. I like having just one. Harriet.

LUISA: Harriet said you and Clare needed me.

ANA: We do. It's awful hearing Harriet throw up after chemo. I hate it. So does Clare. And it'll be better if you're home. But not if you're always mad at me for not speaking Spanish. And not if you're not nice to Brian.

LUISA: *(Sighs and rolls her eyes)* Brian. *(Beat)* You know, I was really glad to see her.

ANA: Who?

LUISA: Harriet. I missed her. A lot.

ANA: You should tell her.

(Dan's Uncertainty Reprise *[Track 10] closes the scene and opens scene 11.)*

Scene 11 (June: Two months later)

(HARRIET's kitchen. LUISA and ANITA are sitting at the island stuffing Global Family *newsletters into envelopes.)*

ANITA: *(Upset)* I didn't know.

LUISA: *(Surprised)* How could you not know?

ANITA: I don't know. I was busy. We stopped talking . . .

LUISA: None of the other Globals said anything?

ANITA: No. They must not know either.

LUISA: *(Angry)* How is it that none of the Globals know that Harriet has breast cancer? Did everyone cut her off?

ANITA: *(Defensive)* We didn't cut her off. She cut us off!

LUISA: Did you ever try to call her after that disagreement about Seder?

ANITA: Of course. *(Beat)* Once or twice.

LUISA: *(Angry)* Once or twice! You were close friends. She was the one who hosted all those Global Family parties. Why didn't you try harder?

ANITA: *(Defensive)* How hard did you try? You're the one who took off to Colombia when you found out about . . .

LUISA: Marty.

ANITA: Marty. What kind of name is that for a woman?

LUISA: I didn't leave because of Marty. I left to find my mother. And I didn't stop speaking to her. I spoke to her every Sunday. Just like before.

ANITA: And did you tell the Sisters all about your mother's new girlfriend?

LUISA: *(Hesitates, then)* No.

ANITA: It's not so easy, is it?

LUISA: But I didn't cut her off and I came back when she needed me.

ANITA: *(Sincere)* And I'm sure she's very glad to have you home.

LUISA: You need to apologize.

ANITA: What?

LUISA: We still don't know if they got it all. Or if the cancer will come back. If it does, we'll need help from you and the other Globals. You need to apologize so you can become friends again.

ANITA: I tried calling. She never returned my calls.

LUISA: She says you rejected her.

ANITA: I didn't reject her.

LUISA: Well, she thinks you did.

ANITA: Well, that's her problem. Tell me about you. Have you started fundraising?

LUISA: *(Decides to allow ANITA to change the topic for the moment)* I'm strategizing. I went to the see the people at the Stephen Lewis Foundation. They raise money to support children affected by HIV and AIDS in Africa.

ANITA: I know what they do.

LUISA: I like their philosophy. *(Careful, trying to avoid an argument)* They think that one of the best ways to help children is to support the orphanages in a way that allows them to stay in their own countries.

ANITA: *(Annoyed).* I hate all that talk about how bad it is to take children out of their country, out of their culture. They live in an orphanage, for God's sake. They have no culture.

LUISA: You know that's not true. Ana and I learned to read and write in Spanish in the orphanage. We sang songs, played games. When we came here, we lost a lot of that.

ANITA: You can't tell me that growing up in an orphanage is better than growing up in a family.

LUISA: I know.

(There's an awkward silence.)

ANITA: So how long are you planning to stay?

LUISA: I'm not sure. I'm thinking of going back to school. Marty says I should use the privileged middle-class life Harriet gave me to go to medical school so I can set up the clinic we're building.

ANITA: *(Annoyed again)* She didn't just give you a "privileged middle-class life." She gave you and Ana a loving home. A family. She gave you a mother!

LUISA: We didn't need a mother. We already had one.

ANITA: No you didn't. Your mother had died.

LUISA: But we didn't know she died. To us, she was still alive. And because she was alive in my mind, Harriet could never be my mother. She was just a woman, a very nice woman, who was taking care of Ana and me until we were old enough to take care of ourselves and find our real mother. I never wanted to be Harriet's daughter. All I ever wanted was to go back to Bogotá so I could find my own mother and be her daughter.

ANITA: *(Angry)* I don't understand you.

LUISA: Well, Marty does.

ANITA: Is that so?

LUISA: Marty says it doesn't matter that I never wanted to be Harriet's daughter. What matters is that when Harriet needed me, I came back. That's what daughters do.

(ANITA doesn't respond.)

And that's what good friends do. She needs you back.

(ANITA takes a look at her watch.)

ANITA: What time did you say she was coming back?

LUISA: Five.

ANITA: And she knows I'm here.

LUISA: She knows.

ANITA: And she'll be happy to see me.

LUISA: If you apologize.

ANITA: It's been such a long time. What do I say?

LUISA: Hi. It's good to see you. I'm sorry you've been sick.

ANITA: You make it sound so easy.

(Offstage, HARRIET and MARTY are talking and are about to enter. HARRIET is still wearing a bandana that covers her bald head.)

ANITA: *(Looks at her watch)* She's early!

(HARRIET and MARTY enter carrying grocery bags.)

LUISA: *(Gets up)* Hi. Let me help you. *(Takes the bags from HARRIET)*. Marty, this is Anita Levinson from Global Family.

MARTY: Hi.

ANITA: *(Too loud)* Hello. *(Softer)* Hello.

LUISA: We're stuffing newsletters.

HARRIET: Just like old times.

ANITA: Hi. It's good to see you. I'm sorry you've been sick.

HARRIET: *(Guarded)* Thank you. *(To LUISA)* There are more bags in the car.

LUISA: I'll help Marty bring them in.

HARRIET: Thanks.

(HARRIET sits down. MARTY and LUISA leave. ANITA tears up. HARRIET stares at her.)

ANITA: I'm sorry. It's such a shock. To see you so pale, with that schmatte on your head.

HARRIET: I didn't want a wig. They're too hot.

(ANITA nods.)

So.

ANITA: So.

HARRIET: I'm really pissed off at you.

ANITA: *(More vulnerable than angry)* I'm really pissed off at you.

HARRIET: What?

ANITA: You never returned my calls.

HARRIET: You never apologized. I'm waiting for an apology.

ANITA: For what? Not inviting you to Seder? That was over a year ago.

HARRIET: For deserting me. And the girls. Just when we needed you most.

ANITA: You put me in a terrible position.

HARRIET: What?

ANITA: You made me choose between you and the agency.

HARRIET: That's ridiculous.

ANITA: If I condoned your relationship with Marty and the Sisters in Colombia had found out, they would have cut us off. They would have found another agency to work with.

HARRIET: Bullshit.

ANITA: Easy for you to say.

HARRIET: We visited the Sisters. All of us. As a family. They met Marty and they liked her. No one cut us off.

ANITA: They liked her?

HARRIET: Of course they liked her. They admired her. She's the one who kept our family grounded during the surgery, through the chemo. After you abandoned us. *(Beat) (Raw with anger, sadness, regret, loss)* The irony would have been funny if it hadn't hurt so fucking much. The same woman who has dedicated her life to finding homes and families for abandoned children, abandoned one of the families she helped create.

ANITA: *(Shocked, then)* I'm sorry. I'm very sorry.

(Dan's Reconciliation and Reggaetón *[Track 11] begins, closes the scene and opens scene 12.)*

HARRIET: All right, then.

ANITA: *(Reaches out her hand)* Let's start again. Tell me about Marty.

Scene 12 (June: A week later)

(HARRIET's kitchen. Colombian reggaetón opens the scene. HARRIET, MARTY, LUISA and ANA are all sorting clothes to send to the orphanage. ANA is dancing to the music while she sorts the clothes. The music fades.)

LUISA: You want to get married?

HARRIET: Yes.

CLARE/LUISA: Can I be a bridesmaid?/Why?

ANA: Why do straight people get married? For love.

MARTY: And for legitimacy. Getting married will give us legitimacy.

LUISA: You mean as a couple?

MARTY: Yeah.

LUISA: You think?

HARRIET: You don't?

LUISA: No.

ANA: *(Sarcastic)* That's supportive.

LUISA: She asked me what I thought. People who support queer families support queer families. People who don't, don't. Getting married won't make a difference.

ANA: Well, I think it's great you want to get married.

CLARE: Me too!

HARRIET: I'm glad.

LUISA: What's wrong with the way things are now?

MARTY: I didn't like the way one of the nurses treated me when we went in for chemotherapy. She treated me like dirt.

CLARE: What did she say?

MARTY: It doesn't matter now. But, God forbid, if Harriet ever has to be admitted to the hospital, being married will give me some authority in decision-making.

LUISA: You think so?

MARTY: I do.

LUISA: Then you should get married.

HARRIET: *(A little shy)* Would you be my witness?

LUISA: *(Touched)* Sure. Why not?

ANA: *(To MARTY)* And can I be yours?

MARTY: If you're old enough, I'd love you to be mine. We'll find out.

CLARE: And I'll be the bridesmaid.

HARRIET: What about holding the rings for us?

CLARE: Sure!

ANA: You better not lose them.

CLARE: I won't. *(Beat)* We should have a party.

ANA: We should totally have a party. With lots of food and music and dancing. We could invite all the Globals.

HARRIET: We can have a party. And we can invite the Globals and *(rueful)* see who comes. But first, there's one more thing we have to talk about. *(Hesitates)* It's about what happens if I get sick again.

ANA: *(Freaks out)* The cancer's back?

CLARE: *(Scared)* You're sick again?

HARRIET: No, no, no. It's not back. But we need to talk about what's going to happen if it does come back. And if . . .

LUISA: *(Soft)* You don't make it.

HARRIET: Yes.

ANA: *(Gets up to leave the room)* I'm not talking about this.

LUISA: We have to talk about this. Don't be such a baby.

ANA: Shut up!

CLARE: *(Upset)* Don't fight. Please don't fight.

MARTY: Listen. We're going to do everything we can to make sure the cancer doesn't come back. And if it does, then we'll fight it. We'll fight it hard. Just like this time. But we need to figure out who's going to be your guardian in case—

LUISA: I'm nineteen. I don't need a guardian.

HARRIET: No. You don't. But Ana and Clare do. We've talked to your father and—

ANA: I'm not going to live with Jonathon.

CLARE: Me neither.

HARRIET: *(Quick)* You won't have to. Marty wants to be your guardian.

MARTY: *(Quick)* If it's all right with you. And Luisa.

ANA: It's fine with us. And it's fine with Luisa.

LUISA: No, it's not.

ANA: *(Freaks out)* What!

LUISA: I mean, I'm not sure. I need to think about it. It's a big decision.

MARTY: *(Expecting this)* Right.

LUISA: Maybe I could be Ana's guardian. And you could be Clare's.

MARTY: *(Careful)* Maybe.

CLARE: I'll still see Daddy every summer at the cottage, right?

MARTY: Of course. Every summer.

ANA: *(To Luisa)* It's my decision, not yours. And I want Marty to be my guardian.

LUISA: But I'm your sister.

ANA: Yeah, my sister. Not my mother.

HARRIET: Look we don't have to decide right this minute. I'm planning to be around for a long time so that no one will need a guardian. This is just in case. *(Takes MARTY hand)* Let's just leave this for now and go out for dinner. To celebrate.

(She gives MARTY a kiss.)

Where do you want to go?

ANA: The Keg.

LUISA: I hate The Keg. All that meat, it's disgusting. There's nothing for vegetarians.

ANA: It's not disgusting. And you can have a salad.

LUISA: I hate having to order a salad just because there's nothing else.

HARRIET: Yeah, I hear you.

LUISA: Let's go to Fresh.

ANA: But if we go to The Keg we can order a cake. And it will come with sparklers and the waiters will sing and it will be a real celebration.

HARRIET: Clare?

CLARE: Mexican.

ANA: You always say Mexican.

LUISA: What's wrong with Mexican?

ANA: Nothing. I just want to go to The Keg.

HARRIET: We'll let Marty choose.

MARTY: No way. I'm not choosing. You choose.

HARRIET: Let's just go. We'll decide in the van. Whose got the keys?

MARTY: Me. Let's go, girls.

CLARE: It's my turn to sit near the window.

ANA: No it's not. You sat near the window last time.

(MARTY and the girls exit arguing. HARRIET takes moment to tidy up the table before leaving. Then follows them out. Dan's Reggaetón Bows *[Track 12] closes the scene. Lights fade.* Reggaetón Bows *stays on for bows and applause.)*

End of play

Post-show music

(After the bows Dan Parker's Reggaetón Closing [Track 13] begins.)

Acknowledgments

I want to thank and acknowledge the participants I interviewed for the Harriet's House project and the writers and filmmakers of the texts I worked with during the research and writing phase of Harriet's House. Their perspectives appear in the script and in this book. I also want to acknowledge Amy Gullage, Monica Nunes, Dan Parker, and Manu Sharma for their research and production assistance. The Social Sciences and Humanities Research Council of Canada funded the research: first through its Small Institutional Grants program, and then through its Standard Research Grant program. The Department of Curriculum, Teaching and Learning at the Ontario Institute for Studies in Education, University of Toronto provided institutional support of the project.

Texts consulted

Bonkowski, B. (2005). *Jesse's World: A Story of Adoption and the Global Family*. Milsons Point (Sydney), NSW: Random House Australia.

Boluda, A. (Director/Producer) (2005). *Queer Spawn*. NY/Barcelona: Anna Boluda.

Casper, V., and Schultz, S. (1999). *Gay Parents/Straight Schools: Building Communication and Trust*. New York: Teacher's College Press.

Eng, D.L. (2006) Political economies of passion: Transnational adoption and global studies. *Gender and Sexuality*, 7(1):49–59.

Eng, David L. (2003). Transnational adoption and queer diasporas. *Social Text 21* (3):1–37.

Eng, David L., and Han, S. (2006). Desegregating love transnational adoption, racial reparation, and racial transitional objects. *Studies in Gender and Sexuality* 7 (2):141–172.

Jacobson, H. (2008). *Culture Keeping: White Mothers, International Adoption, and the Negotiation of Family Difference*. Nashville: Vanderbilt University Press.

Kennedy, R. (2003). *Interracial Intimacies: Sex, Marriage, Identity, and Adoption*. New York: Pantheon.

Opper, Nicole. (Director/Producer) (2009). *Off and Running: An American Coming of Age Story*. NY: Nicole Opper Productions.

Register, Cheri (2005). *Beyond Good Intentions: A Mother Reflects on Raising Internationally Adopted Children*. St. Paul, MN: Yeong and Yeong.

Trenka, J. Jeong, Oparah, J. Chinyere, and Sun,Yung Shin (Eds.) (2006). *Outsiders Within: Writing on Transracial Adoption*. Cambridge, MA: South End Press.

Turner Strong, P. (2001) To forget their tongue, their Name, and their whole relation. In S. Franklin and S. McKinnon, (Eds.), *Relative Values: Reconfiguring Kinship Studies* (pp. 468–93). Durham and London: Duke University Press.

Vonk, E. (2001) Cultural competence for transracial adoptive parents, *Social Work* 46(3) 246–255.

APPENDIX B

BIOGRAPHIES FOR THE CAST AND ARTISTIC TEAM FOR *HARRIET'S HOUSE*

Cast

Rebecca Applebaum (Ana)
Rebecca Applebaum is a Toronto actor, playwright and musician.

Julie Burris (Marty)
Julie's previous acting credits include *Mary Stuart* (East Side Players), *The Uninvited* (Scarborough Theatre Guild), *Iphigenia at her Funeral* (Alumnae Festival 2009), *Point of Viewing* (Queen Elizabeth Dinner Theatre), and *Pound Predators* (Gailey Road Productions).

Estée Feldman (Clare)
Estée Feldman is a high school student in Toronto. In 2009, Estée was cast in a play by Molière at The Toronto French School and attended a course at Second City. In 2010, she attended the Randolph Academy.

Joanne Latimer (Harriet)
Joanne Latimer (Equity/Actra) is a Toronto-area actor and teacher who is committed to equity issues and good theatre. Theatre credits include *That Summer* (4th Line Theatre), *Snapshot* (Toronto; London; New York/Cygnet

Theatre) and *Tony and Tina's Wedding* (Second City Toronto). Her recent film and television credits include *Me and Luke* and *Living in Your Car*.

Jorie Morrow (Anita)
Jorie Morrow is a graduate of George Brown College Theatre School. Theatre credits include: Hanna Kennedy in *Mary Stuart* with Eastside Players, Amanda Wingfield in *The Glass Menagerie*, and Miss Maudie in *To Kill A Mockingbird* both with Scarborough Players.

Supinder Wraich (Luisa)
Supinder Wraich graduated from the University of Ottawa with a Bachelor of Arts degree in Communications. She works in Toronto as an actor and has appeared on the big screen alongside Jason Lewis (*Sex and the City*) and Eric McCormack (*Will and Grace*). Her small screen credits include appearances on the hit TV show *Degrassi The Next Generation*, as well as a reoccurring role on the CBC television series *The Border*. On computer screen, she stars in the upcoming webseries *Guidestones*. *Harriet' s House* marked Supinder' s debut on a Toronto stage with an ensemble cast.

Artistic team

Wade Gamble
Lighting Designer
A performer from Victoria, British Columbia, Wade has worked across Canada with Theatre Aquarius, Citadel Theatre, Silvermist Productions, and Chemainus Theatre. Past lighting designs include *Grief: Another Common Bond* (Fayez1Productions), *Putting It Together* (ASNY), *Goodnight Desdemona, Good-morning Juliet* (CCPA), and *City of Angels*-pt.1&2 (wheresnoonan). Wade is a graduate of the Canadian College of Performing Arts.

Jake Goldstein
Photographer and videographer
Jake Goldstein is a high school student in Toronto. *Harriet's House* is his first photography and videography project for a theatrical production.

Tara Goldstein
Founder, Artistic Director of Gailey Road Productions, Playwright and Producer of *Harriet's House*
Tara Goldstein is a playwright, producer and a professor of education at the Ontario Institute of Studies in Education at the University of Toronto.

She graduated from the MFA Playwriting Program at Spalding University, Louisville, Kentucky, in November 2006 and then founded Gailey Road Productions, a theatre company that produces women-centred research-informed theatre in July 2007. Tara's historical drama *Lost Daughter* won the 2005 Canadian Jewish Playwriting Contest and was produced by Gailey Road at the 2008 Toronto Fringe Festival. Her play *Pound Predators*, a parody about "the war against weight," was produced at the 2007 Toronto Fringe Festival. Tara's latest project *Harriet's House*, a contemporary drama about transnational adoption in a same-sex family, was produced at Hart House Theatre in July 2010. In addition to her work for the stage, Tara has written seven research-based plays on the schooling of minority high school and university students, which have been used in university and high school classrooms across Canada, the United States and Australia. A monologue from *Hong Kong, Canada* has been published in Judith Thompson's (2004) *She Speaks: Monologues for Women* and a ten-minute play called *Seder* appears in *The Hollow and Other Plays: A Collection of Plays from the New Play Development Workshop 2004–2007*. In June 2010 Tara became the chair of the Women's Caucus of the Playwright's Guild of Canada.

Esther Kim
Production Designer
Esther Kim is a recent graduate of Ryerson Theatre School's technical production program, with a background in studio arts and art history. Her work has been featured Markham Regional Theatre, Abrams Studio Theatre and Ryerson Mainstage. Recent work includes *Chester Mystery Cycles* at Victoria College, University of Toronto and *Double Double*, at Theatre Passe-Muraille, 2010 Toronto Fringe Festival.

Gillian Lewis
Production Manager of Gailey Road Productions and *Harriet's House*
Gillian Lewis is a freelance production manager and stage manager for various theatrical and dance companies in Toronto. Recent credits include: assistant stage manager for the National Ballet of Canada's 2010 *Sleeping Beauty and Nutcracker*, stage manager for *Small Wooden Shoes Dedicated to the Revolutions*, production stage manager for Fallen Rock's *The 25th Annual Putnam County Spelling Bee* and Stage Manager for the National Ballet of Canada's *YOU Dance* performances. Gillian has been with Gailey Road since its creation. She stage-managed its first two productions, *Pound Predators* and *Lost Daughter*, and was production manager for *Harriet's House*.

Tara Mohan
Stage Manager
Tara Mohan is currently studying at Ryerson University where she has worked on a number of productions in varied roles, including production stage manager of *Ryerson Dances 2011*, and stage manager *Choreographic Works 2010*. Recent credits include: stage manager of George Brown Dance's *Spring Showcase 2011*, assistant stage manager of Teatron Jewish Theatre's *A Hamburger in a Pita*, and stage manager of The Dance Migration's *Os Elementos*.

Monica Nunes
Intern of Gailey Road Productions and Assistant Producer of *Harriet's House*
Monica Nunes graduated from the Masters of Public Health program at the University of Toronto specializing in health promotion and community development. She is interested in using theatre and performance to disseminate research in the area of health education, and used her internship with Gailey Road Productions to learn more about the creation and production of research-informed theatre.

Dan Parker
Sound Designer
Dan Parker graduated from Carleton University and the University of Toronto with a Bachelors degree in Humanities and a Bachelors degree in Education, respectively. He is a musician, singer, songwriter and high school teacher. He has sung in many rock groups and is currently fronting FP2: www.myspace.com/fpdeux. Along with singing in the choir of Orchestre Symphonique de Québec, he also competes in the Music Improv League of Trois Rivières. The sound design for *Harriet's House* was performed, recorded and produced by Dan Parker using only his voice.

Lisa Rupchand
Graphic Designer
Lisa Rupchand graduated from the University of Toronto with an honours bachelor of arts degree, majoring in English and philosophy. She currently works in the field of educational administration at OISE/UT but has developed a particular interest in print design, and made the decision a few years ago to pursue graphic and publication design at a professional level. Lisa assisted in the program design for Gailey Road's second production, *Lost Daughter*.

Jocelyn Wickett

Artistic Director of Gailey Road Productions and Director of *Harriet's House*

Jocelyn Wickett is currently teaching drama at Jarvis Collegiate in Toronto, completing her MA at the University of Toronto, and working with Gailey Road Productions as Artistic Director. A graduate of the *Theatre Performance Program* at Concordia University in Montreal, Jocelyn has been working as an actor, dancer, choreographer, teacher and director for the ten years. She has experience in classical, contemporary, and musical theatre, as well as issue-based theatre, theatre of the oppressed, collective creation and performed ethnography. *Harriet's House* is the third play that Jocelyn has directed for Gailey Road Productions. Previous credits with the company include: *Lost Daughter* (2008), *Pound Predators* (2007) and two staged readings of *Zero Tolerance*.

APPENDIX C

A SELECTED BIBLIOGRAPHY ON RESEARCH-INFORMED THEATRE

Brown, Paul (Ed.) (2010) *Verbatim: Staging Memory and Community*. Strawberry Hill, New South Wales: Currency Press.

Provides an overview of Australian verbatim and documentary theatre practices and an analysis of one American and four Australian research-informed plays: *The Laramie Project* by Moisés Kaufman and The Tectonic Theatre; *Aftershocks* by Paul Brown; *Minefields and Miniskirts* by Terence O'Connell, *Parramatta Girls* by Alana Valentine, and *Run Rabbit Run* by Alana Valentine.

Conquergood, Dwight. (2003). Performing as a Moral Act: Ethical Dimensions of Ethnography in Performance. In Y. Lincoln & N. Denzin (Eds.), *Turning Points in Qualitative Research: Tying Knots in a Handkerchief* (pp. 397–413). Walnut Creek, CA: AltaMira.

Identifies four ethical pitfalls in writing and staging research-informed theatre: The Custodian's Rip-Off, where research participants are denigrated for purposes of entertainment; The Enthusiast's Infatuation, where the experiences of research participants are trivialized; The Curator's Exhibitionism, where cultural differences are over-emphasized and The Skeptic's Cop-Out, where realism is sacrificed for sensationalism.

Denzin, Norman. (2003). *Performance Ethnography: Critical Pedagogy and the Politics of Culture*. Thousand Oaks: Sage.

Outlines a theoretical foundation for performance ethnography and provides American examples including memoir, essays, short story and autoethnography. Also examines the particular ethics and practical politics associated with the writing of autoethnography.

Favorini, Antillio (Ed.) (1995). *Voicings: Ten Plays and a Scenario from Documentary Theatre*. New Jersey: Ecco Press.

Provides an overview of British and American documentary theatre practices and argues that documentary theatre is highly relevant in societies that aggressively create and consume contemporary news. Includes ten examples of 20th century documentary theatre: *In Spite of Everything!* (Erwin Piscator and Felix Gasbarra); *Ethiopia* (Arthur Arent); *World on Edge* (Eric Paige and Roger Woddis); *The Investigation* (Peter Weiss); *Inquest* (Donald Freed); *Fight for Shelton Bar* (Peter Cheeseman [et al.]); *Quilters* (Molly Newman and Barbara Damashek); *Execution of Justice* (Emily Mann); *Compensation* (Sergei Kurginian) and *Unquestioned Integrity* by Mame Hunt.

Goldstein, Tara, with Jocelyn Wickett. (2009). *Zero Tolerance*: A Stage Adaptation of an Investigative Report on School Safety. *Qualitative Inquiry* 15(10): 1552–1568.

Discusses the task of adapting a Canadian investigative report on school safety into a performance for the stage, providing a model for how research-informed theatre artists can assist in the dissemination of other researchers' research and investigative reports.

Goldstein, Tara (2008). Performed Ethnography: Possibilities, Multiple Commitments, and the Pursuit of Rigour. In K. Gallagher (Ed.), *The Methodological Dilemma: Critical, Creative, and Post-Positivist Approaches to Qualitative Research*. New York: Routledge, 85–102.

Argues that performed ethnography is characterized by multiple commitments to ethnography, drama and critical discussion which sometimes lie in tension with each other and present ethical dilemmas for the researcher. Includes a discussion of how work from American and Canadian feminist theatre can provide a model for honouring multiple commitments.

Mann, Emily (1996). *Testimonies: Four Plays*. New York: Theatre Communications Group.

Includes four examples of Emily Mann's historical drama work about the Holocaust (*Annulla*); the Vietnam War (*Still Life*); the assassination of San Francisco's mayor and openly gay supervisor (*Execution of Justice*), and the 1979 North Carolina riot in which an anti-Klan rally turned into a Klan killing spree (*Greensboro: A Requiem*).

Mienczakowski, Jim, and Teresa Moore. (2008). Performing Data with Notions of Responsibility. *Handbook of the Arts in Qualitative Research*. In J. Gary Knowles and Ardra L. Cole (Eds.), London: Sage Publications, 451–458.

Discusses ethical issues that accompany the creation of research-informed theatre and offers a set of guiding practices to ensure that researchers "do no harm" in researching, writing and performing research-informed theatre.

Prendergast, Monica (Ed.) (2010). Special Issue on Research-Based Applied Theatre. *Canadian Journal of Practice-Based Research in Theatre*, 2(1).

Includes an introduction on practice-based and applied theatre research (Monica Prendergast), a research-based script about aging and driving by Warwick Dobson called *No Particular Place to Go* and three reflection essays about writing and performing the script: bringing data to life (Trudy Pauluth-Penner), balancing analytic and artistic practices (Lauren Jerke), integrating community-based theatre practices (Yasmine Kandil). Also includes a transcript of a post-show conversation about the play.

Saldaña, Johnny. (Ed.) (forthcoming) *Ethnotheatre: Research from Page to Stage*. Walnut Creek: Left Coast Press.

The book will include an overview of playwriting and production methods for ethnotheatre.

Saldaña, Johnny. (Ed.) (2005). *Ethnodrama: An Anthology of Reality Theatre*. New York: Altamira Press.

Includes an introductory chapter on how to dramatize data and features nine examples of American, Australian and Canadian ethnodramas: *Voices in the Rain* (Micheal Keck), *Scenes from 14* (José Casa); *Chalkboard Concerto: Growing Up as a Teacher in the Chicago Public Schools* (Charles Vanover and Johnny Saldaña); *Storm Tracking: Scenes of Marital Disintegration* (Elissa Foster); *The Practice* (Matthew J. Meyer); *Wearing the Secret Out* (Jennifer Chapman, Anne Swedberg and Heather Sykes); *Baddies, Grubs and the Nitty-Gritty* (Jim Mienczakowski and Steven Morgan); *Street Rat* (Johnny Saldaña, Susan Finley, and Macklin Finley) and *Hidden* (Michael Rohd and Laura Eason with Sojourn Theatre Artists).

Taylor, Philip. (2003). *Applied Theatre: Creating Transformative Encounters in the Community*. New York: Falmer Press.

Discusses how theatre practices can be used to raise awareness, propose alternatives, provide healing and implement change in local communities. Also discusses the ethics of working with applied theatre and evaluating the impact of applied theatre projects.

NOTES

The World of Research-Informed Theatre

1. See Saldaña 2005, pp. 10–14 for examples of work in many of these areas.
2. *Hong Kong, Canada*, a play about immigration and multilingualism in a Canadian high school, is published in Goldstein 2003.
3. See Goldstein 1997 and 2003.
4. See Denzin 2003.
5. See Saldaña 2005.
6. See Mienczakowski and Moore 2008
7. See Mienczakowski and Morgan 1993.
8. See Clifford and Marcus 1986.
9. From Behar 1995, p. 3.
10. See Clifford 1983.
11. From Behar 1995, p. 4.
12. The term "Other people" has been used to refer to people of color who have been marginalized and oppressed. For an example of how this term has been used in education, see Lisa Delpit's (1995) book *Other People's Children: Cultural Conflict in the Classroom.*
13. See Behar and Gordon 1995 and Kondo 1995.
14. From Kondo 1995, p. 52.
15. See Richardson 2000.
16. See Lincoln 1997.
17. See Ensler 1998.

18. See Kaufman and the Techtonic Theatre Project 2001.
19. See Smith 1993 and 1994.
20. Reported in "Twilight: Los Angeles, 1992." *Drama for Students*. Eds. David Galens and Lynn Spampinato. Vol. 2. Detroit: Gale, 1998, pp. 233–253.
21. From Smith 1994.
22. For more information about the Gotham Writing Workshop see www.writingclasses.com
23. See Glow 2007.
24. See Solomon 2001.
25. See Goldstein 2000.
26. See McIntosh 1999 for a description of the some of the ideas we worked with.
27. See Ellis 1997.
28. *Snakes and Ladders* is published in the *International Journal of Curriculum and Pedagogy* (see Goldstein 2010). For further discussion on teaching with *Snakes and Ladders*, a play about challenging homophobia in a Canadian high school, see Goldstein 2005.
29. For more information about the MFA in Playwriting program at Spalding see www.spalding.edu/academics/mfa/
30. *Pound Predators* and *Lost Daughter* are available on T-Space, the University of Toronto's Research Repository, which can be accessed on web with the following address: https://tspace.library.utoronto.ca
31. See Brown 2010 and Saldaña 2005 for a discussion on the term "reality theatre."
32. From the Preface of *The Cambridge Companion to Caryl Churchill* (Aston and Diamond 2009).
33. See Churchill 1982.
34. See Reinelt 2009.
35. From Reinelt 2009, p. 30.
36. From Reinelt 2009, p. 31.
37. See Churchill 1982.
38. See Mann 1997.
39. From Wake 2010, p. 8.
40. *Zero Tolerance* is available on T-Space, the University of Toronto's Research Repository, which can be accessed on web with the following address: https://tspace.library.utoronto.ca
41. See Goldstein with Wickett 2009.
42. See Brown 2010.
43. From Brown 2010, pp. 2–5.
44. From Brown 2010, pp. 81–83.
45. From Brown 2010, pp. 109–112.
46. See Mienczakowski and Moore 2008.
47. From Wake 2010, pp. 6–8.
48. See Martin 2006.
49. The description of *The Execution of Justice* as a documentary play appears in chapter three of Paul Brown's *Verbatim: Staging Memory and Community* (see Brown 2010, p. 14).
50. I saw a production of *I, Elizabeth*, featuring playwright Rebecca Vaughan as Queen Elizabeth at the Adelaide Fringe Festival in March 2011. As far as I know, the script has not been published. To inquire about obtaining a copy of the script, contact Guy Masterson, Artistic Director of The Centre for International Theatre at guy@citadelaide.com

Writing and Workshopping *Harriet's House*

1. See Garrison 2001.
2. The texts I worked with both before, during and after the reading group meetings included Boluda 2005; Casper and Schultz 1999; Eng 2003, 2006; Eng and Han 2006; Gray 2009; Jacobson 2008; Kennedy 2003; Opper 2009; Rafkin 1990; Register 2005; Trenka 2009, 2005; Trenka, Oparah, and Sun 2006; Turner Strong 2001 and Vonk 2001.
3. See Richardson 2000.
4. See Forester 1927.
5. To read the first scenes that were produced from the scene-by-scene outline, see Appendix A.
6. See Register 2005.
7. Each member of the workshop team signed a released form to give me permission to use the audiotapes and videotape texts for "script development and archival purposes."
8. Being "out" (in this case as a same-sex transnationally adoptive family) is a short-hand expression for being "out of the closet" and not hiding the fact that one is living in a same-sex family.
9. Harriet adopts Luisa and Ana and gives birth to Clare while she is married to Jonathon. She meets Marty several years later after she has separated from Jonathon.
10. See López 1996.
11. See http://www.josefinalopez.com.
12. See Volkman 2003, p. 4.
13. See Rebellato 2009, p. 171.
14. Personal e-mail correspondence, May 3, 2011.
15. Personal e-mail correspondence, May 17, 2011.
16. For a powerful examples of work from the new adoption studies see Trenka 2009, 2005; and Trenka, Oparah & Shin 2006.
17. See Trenka, Oparah & Shin 2006.
18. For an excellent analysis of how adoptees' return narratives challenge the idea that returning "home" to their birth country is necessarily vital to their identity construction and well-being see Australian sociologist's Kim Gray's work on Australian adoptees in Gray 2009.
19. See Register 2005, p. 48
20. See Lincoln 1997.

Assessing Research-Informed Theatre and *Harriet's House*

1. See Richardson 2000, p. 937.
2. See Ellis 2000, p. 275.
3. See Denzin 2003, p. 124.
4. See Glow 2007, p. 5. The eight playwrights Hilary Glow interviewed for *Power Plays: Australian Theatre and the Public Agenda* are Andrew Bovell, Patricia Cornelius, Reg Cribb, Ben Ellis, Wesley Enoch, Hannie Rayson, Stephen Sewell, and Katherine Thomson. Sewell began writing in the 1970s; Bovell, Rayson, Thomson and Corneilus in the 1980s; and Enoch, Ellis and Cribb in the late 1990s.

5. See Rayson 2000.
6. See Glow 2007, p. 11.
7. See Glow 2007, p. 11.
8. See Glow 2007, pp. 84–85 and Ellis 2003.
9. See chapter one and Goldstein 2004 for writing on teaching with *Hong Kong, Canada*.
10. See Goldstein 2005 for writing on teaching with *Snakes and Ladders*.
11. Ontario Arts Council Theatre Projects Grant Application submitted by Tara Goldstein on behalf of Gailey Road Productions, September 2010.
12. It's interesting to compare Laurel Richardson's questions about aesthetic merit with Jim Mienczakowski and Teresa Moore's argument that ethnodrama is different from traditional theatrical work. As discussed in chapter one, Mienczakowski and Moore describe ethnodrama as a new aesthetic that values the accurate interpretation of research findings *over* the style, mode, and traditions of theatrical presentation (emphasis is mine). Richardson's questions about aesthetic merit emerge from aesthetic ideals developed in the performing arts. In using Richardson's criteria for assessing creative analytic practice, I am choosing to value traditions of theatrical presentation as well as rigorous interpretation of research findings.
13. See Ellis 2000, p. 273.
14. Bochner 2000, p. 271.
15. See Glow 2007, p. 89 and On 2003.
16. See Glow 2007, p. 89 and Herbert 2003.
17. See Glow 2007, p. 89 and Gray 2003.
18. Personal communication June 16, 2011.
19. Personal communication June 7, 2011.
20. Personal communication June 7, 2011.
21. From the Mothers at the Margins conference program 2011. The conference was held at the University of Queensland from April 27–30, 2011.
22. See Behar 1993, p. xii.
23. See Behar 1993, p. 20.
24. See Behar 1993, p. 20.
25. For an overview of epistemologies in social science research see Anfara and Mertz 2006 and Philips and Burbules 2000.
26. See Ellis 2000, p. 275.
27. See Bochner 2000, p. 271.
28. See Ellis 2000, p. 275.
29. See Denzin 2003, pp. 123–124.

Producing *Harriet's House*

1. See the Hart House Theatre website (www.harthousetheatre.ca).
2. See Wallis 2005.
3. From Seabright 2010, p. 78.
4. From Seabright 2010, p. 72.

5. From Seabright 2010, pp. 82–83.
6. See Crystal 2010.
7. From Seabright 2010, p. 148.
8. From Seabright 2010, pp. 149–155.
9. From Seabright 2010, pp. 151–152.
10. From Seabright 2010, p. 152.
11. From Seabright 2010, p. 156.
12. From Seabright 2010, p. 158.
13. See Denzin 2008, Denzin and Lincoln 2011, Goodall 2008, Pelias 2011, and Richardson 2007 for examples of this work.

Questions and Answers about *Harriet's House*, Research-Informed Theatre and Arts-Based Research

1. See Gray, Sinding, Ivonoffski, Fitch, Hampson and Greenberg 2000 for a description of this collaboration.
2. See Theatre Communications Group 2010.
3. See Leavy 2008.
4. See Knowles and Cole 2008. For other recent work on arts-based research methodologies see Finley 2003 and Siegesmund and Cahnmann-Taylor 2007.
5. See Leavy 2008, p. 12.
6. See Sinner, Leggo, Irwin, Gouzousasis, and Grauer 2006, p. 1238, which is referred to in Leavy 2008, p. 4.
7. See Leavy 2008, p. 14.
8. See Mienczakowski and Moore 2008.
9. See Richardson 2000.
10. See Leavy 2008, p. 17.
11. See Sykes and Goldstein 2004.
12. See Sinner Leggo, Irwin, Gouzousasis, and Grauer 2006.
13. See Cammarota and Fine 2008.
14. See Lather and Smithie 1997.
15. See Knowles and Cole 2008.
16. See Sinner, Leggo, Irwin, Gouzousasis, and Grauer 2006.
17. See Denzin 2002, p. 256.
18. See Denzin 2003 and 2008.
19. See Ellis 2009 and 2004.
20. See Bochner and Ellis 2002.
21. See Pelias 2004 and 2011.
22. I worked with interviews by Marty Moss-Coane in Kolin and Kullman 1996 (Hwang); Jackson Bryer in Bryer 1988 (Hwang); David Savran in Savran 1999 (Kushner and Vogel) and Savran 1988 (Wilson) and Suzan-Lori Parks in Parks 2005 (Wilson).

REFERENCES

Anfara, V. A., and Mertz, N. T. (Eds.). (2006). *Theoretical Frameworks in Qualitative Research*. Thousand Oaks, CA: Sage.

Aston, E., and Diamond, E. (Eds.). (2009). *The Cambridge Companion to Caryl Churchill*. Cambridge: Cambridge University Press.

Behar, R. (1995). Introduction: Out of exile. In R. Behar and D. Gordon (Eds.), *Women Writing Culture* (pp. 1–29). Berkeley: University of California Press.

Behar, R., and Gordon, D. (Eds.). (1995). *Women Writing Culture*. Berkeley: University of California Press.

Behar, R. (1993). *Translated Woman: Crossing the Border with Esperanza's Story*. Boston: Beacon Press.

Bochner, A. (2000). Criteria against ourselves. *Qualitative Inquiry* 6:266–72.

Bochner, A., and Ellis, C. (Eds.). (2002). *Ethnographically Speaking: Autoethnography, Literature & Aesthetics*. Walnut Creek, CA: AltaMira Press.

Boluda, A. (Director/Producer) (2005). *Queer Spawn*. NY/Barcelona: Anna Boluda.

Bonkowski, B. (2005). *Jesse's World: A Story of Adoption and the Global Family*. Milsons Point, NSW (Sydney): Random House Australia.

Brown, P. (Ed.) (2010). *Verbatim: Staging Memory and Community*. Strawberry Hills, NWS: Currency Press.

Bryer, J. R. (1998). David Henry Hwang. In *The Playwright's Art: Conversations with Contemporary American Dramatists*. New Brunswick, NJ: Rutgers University Press.

Cammarota, J., and Fine, M. (Eds.). (2008) *Revolutionizing Education: Youth Participatory Action Research in Motion*. New York: Routledge Publishers.

Casper, V., and Schultz, S. (1999). *Gay Parents/Straight Schools: Building Communication and Trust*. New York: Teacher's College Press.

Churchill, C. (1982). *Top Girls*. London: Methuen.

Clifford, J. (1983). On ethnographic authority. *Representations*. (1):118–146.

Clifford, J., and Marcus, G. (Eds.). (1986). *Writing Culture: The Poetics and Politics of Ethnography*. Berkeley: University of California Press.

Cooper, B. (2009). *Innocence Lost*. Toronto: J. Gorden Shillingford Publishing.

Crystal, L. Tung (2010). Opening the Golden Gate. *American Theatre*. March 2010: 26–29 and 66–69.

Delpit, L. (1995). *Other People's Children: Cultural Conflict in the Classroom*. New York: The New Press.

Denzin, N. (2008). *Searching for Yellowstone: Race, Gender, Family, and Memory in the Postmodern West*. Walnut Creek, CA: Left Coast Press.

Denzin, N. (2003). *Performance Ethnography: Critical Pedagogy and the Politics of Culture*. Thousand Oaks, CA: Sage.

Denzin, N. (2002). Cowboys and Indians. *Symbolic Interaction* 25: 251–261.

Denzin, N. (1997). *Interpretive Ethnography: Ethnographic Practices for the 21st Century*. Thousand Oaks, CA: Sage.

Denzin, N., and Lincoln, Y. S. (2011). *The Sage Handbook of Qualitative Research*. Fourth Edition. Thousand Oaks, CA: Sage.

Ellis, B. (2003). *Falling Petals*. Sydney: Currency Press.

Ellis, C. (2009). *Revision: Autoethnographic Reflections on Life and Work*. Walnut Creek, CA: Left Coast Press.

Ellis, C. (2004). *The Ethnographic I: A Methodological Novel about Autoethnography*, Walnut Creek, CA: AltaMira Press.

Ellis, C. (2000). Creating criteria: An ethnographic short story. *Qualitative Inquiry* 6: 273–77.

Ellis, C. (1997). Evocative Autoethnography: Writing emotionally about our lives. In W.G. Tierney and Y.S. Lincoln (Eds.). *Representation and the Text: Re-framing the Narrative Voice* (pp. 116–139). Albany: SUNY Press.

Eng, D.L. (2006). Political economies of passion: Transnational adoption and global studies. *Gender and Sexuality*, 7(1): 49–59.

Eng, D. L. (2003). Transnational adoption and queer diasporas. *Social Text 21*(3): 1–37.

Eng, D. L., and Han, S. (2006). Desegregating love transnational adoption, racial reparation, and racial transitional objects. *Studies in Gender and Sexuality* 7(2): 141–172.

Ensler, E. (1998). *The Vagina Monologues*. New York: Villard.

Finley, S. (2003). Arts-based inquiry in *QI*: Seven years from crisis to guerrilla warfare. *Qualitative Inquiry* 9(2): 281–296.

Forester, E.M. (1927). *Aspects of the Novel*. New York: Harcourt Brace.

Garrison, G. (2001). *Perfect 10: Writing and Producing the 10-Minute Play*. Portsmouth, NH: Heinemann.

Glow, H. (2007). *Power Plays: Australian Theatre and the Public Agenda*. Sydney: Currency Press.

Goldstein, T. (2010). *Snakes and Ladders*: A performed ethnography. *International Journal of Curriculum and Pedagogy* 3(1): 68–113.

Goldstein, T., with Wickett, J. (2009). Zero Tolerance: A stage adaptation of an investigative report on school safety. *Qualitative Inquiry 15*(10): 1552–1568.

Goldstein, T. (2005). Performed ethnography for anti-homophobia teacher education: Linking research to teaching. *Canadian On-Line Journal of Queer Studies in Education, 1* (1), 25 pages. (http://jqstudies.oise.utoronto.ca/journal/viewarticle.php?id=13&layout)

Goldstein, T. (2004). Performed ethnography for critical language teacher education. In Bonny Norton and Kelleen Toohey (Eds.), *Critical Pedagogies and Language Learning* (pp. 311–326). Cambridge: Cambridge University Press.

Goldstein, T. (2003). *Teaching and Learning in a Multilingual School: Choices, Risks and Dilemmas* (includes the performed ethnography *Hong Kong, Canada*). Mahwah, NJ: Lawrence Erlbaum Associates. With contributions by Gordon Pon and Judith Ngan.

Goldstein, T. (2000). *Hong Kong, Canada*: Performed ethnography for anti-racist teacher education. *Teaching Education Journal. 11*(3): 311–326.

Goldstein, T. (1997). *Two Languages at Work: Bilingual Life on the Production Floor*. New York Berlin: Mouton de Gruyter.

Goodall, H. L. (2008). *Writing Qualitative Inquiry: Self, Stories, and Academic Life*. Walnut Creek, CA: Left Coast Press.

Gray, K. M. (2009). *'Bananas, Bastards and Victims'?: Australian Intercountry Adoptees and Cultural Belonging*. Saarbrucken, Germany: VDM Verlag Dr. Muller.

Gray, P. (2003). Caught in the crossfire. *Herald Sun*. July 21. 116.

Gray, R., Sinding, C., Ivonoffski, V., Fitch, M., Hampson, A., and Greenberg, M. (2000). The use of research-based theatre in a project related to metastatic breast cancer. *Health Expectations* 3(2): 137–44.

Herbert, K. (2003). Bush drama tortured to death. *Herald Sun*. July 4: 90

Jacobson, H. (2008). *Culture Keeping: White Mothers, International Adoption, and the Negotiation of Family Difference*. Nashville: Vanderbilt University Press.

Kaufman, M., and the Tectonic Theater Project. (2001). *The Laramie Project*. New York: Vintage.

Kennedy, R. (2003). *Interracial Intimacies: Sex, Marriage, Identity, and Adoption*. New York: Pantheon.

Knowles, J. Gary, and Cole, Ardra (Eds.). (2008). *Handbook of the Arts in Qualitative Research: Perspectives, Methodologies, Examples, and Issues*. Thousand Oaks, CA: Sage Publications.

Kondo, D. (1995). Bad girls: Theater, women of color, and the politics of representation. In R. Behar and Deborah Gordon (Eds.), *Women Writing Culture* (pp. 49–64). Berkeley: University of California Press.

Lather, P., and Smithies, Chris (1997). *Troubling the Angels: Women Living with HIV/AIDS*. Boulder, CO: Westview/Harper Collins.

Leavy, P. (2008). *Method Meets Art: Arts-Based Research Practice*. New York: Guilford Publications.

Lincoln, Y.S. (1997). Self: subject, audience, text: Living on the edge, writing in the margin. In W. Tierney and Y.S Lincoln (Eds.), *Representation and the Text:* Re-framing the Narrative Voice (pp. 37–55). New York: SUNY Press.

López, J. (1996). *Real Women Have Curves*. Woodstock, IL: The Dramatic Publishing Company.

Mann, E. (1997). *The Execution of Justice*. In *Testimonies: Four Plays* (pp. 133–246). New York: Theatre Communications Group.

Martin, C. (2006). Bodies of evidence. *TDR: The Drama Review*, 50(3), 8–15.

McIntosh, P. (1999). White privilege: Unpacking the invisible knapsack. In: E. Lee, Deborah Menkart and Margo Okazawa-Rey (Eds.), *Beyond Heroes and Holidays: A Practical Guide to K-12 Anti-Racist, Multicultural Education and Staff Development* (pp. 83–86). Washington, DC: Network of Educators on the Americas.

Mienczakowski, J., and Moore, T. (2008). Performing data with notions of responsibility. In J. Gary Knowles and Ardra L. Cole (Eds.), *Handbook of the Arts in Qualitative Research* (pp. 451–458). Thousand Oaks, CA: Sage Publications.

Mienczakowski, J., and Morgan S. (1993). *Busting: The Challenge of the Drought Spirit* (script). Brisbane, Australia: Griffith University Reprographics.

Moss-Coane, M. (1996). David Henry Hwang. In P.C. Kolin and C. H. Kullman (Eds.), *Speaking On Stage: Interviews with Contemporary American Playwrights* (pp. xx). Tuscaloosa: The University of Alabama Press.

On, T. (2003) No easy way out of a dying country town. *Australian*, July 4: 14.

Opper, Nicole (Director/Producer) (2009). *Off and Running: An American Coming of Age Story*. New York: Nicole Opper Productions.

Parks, S.L. (2005). The Light in August. *American Theatre*, November 2005. www.tcg.org/publications/at/nov05/wilson.com

Pelias, R. (2004). *A Methodology of the Heart: Evoking Academic and Daily Life*. Walnut Creek, CA: AltaMira.

Pelias, R. (2011). *Leaning: A Poetics of Personal Relations*. Walnut Creek, CA: Left Coast Press.

Philips, D., and Burbules, N. (2000). *Postpositivism and Educational Research*. Lanham, MD: Rowman and Littlefield.

Rafkin, L. (Ed.). (1990). *Different Mothers: Sons and Daughters of Lesbians Talk about Their Lives*. San Francisco: Cleis Press.

Rayson, H. (2000). *Life After George*. Sydney: Currency Press.

Rebellato, D. (2009). On Churchill's influences. In E. Aston and E. Diamond (Eds.), *The Cambridge Companion to Caryl Churchill* (pp. 163–179). Cambridge: Cambridge University Press.

Register, Cheri (2005). *Beyond Good Intentions: A Mother Reflects on Raising Internationally Adopted Children*. St. Paul, MN: Yeong and Yeong.

Reinelt, J. (2009). On feminist and sexual politics. In E. Aston and E. Diamond (Eds.), *The Cambridge Companion to Caryl Churchill* (pp. 18–35). Cambridge: Cambridge University Press.

Richardson, L. (2007). *Last Writes: A Daybook for a Dying Friend*. Walnut Creek, CA: Left Coast Press.

Richardson, L. (2000). Writing: A method of inquiry. In N. Denzin, and Y.S. Lincoln (Eds.), *Handbook of Qualitative Research* (pp. 723–948). 2nd Edition. Thousand Oaks, CA: Sage.

Saldaña, J. (Ed.) (2005). *Ethnodrama: An Anthology of Reality Theatre*. New York: Altamira Press.

Savran, D. (1999). Tony Kushner. In: *The Playwright's Voice: American Dramatists on Memory, Writing, and the Politics of Culture*. New York: Theatre Communications Group.

Savran, D. (1999). Paula Vogel. In: *The Playwright's Voice: American Dramatists on Memory, Writing, and the Politics of Culture*. New York: Theatre Communications Group.

Savran, D. (1988). August Wilson. In: *In Their Own Words: Contemporary American Playwrights*. New York: Theatre Communications Group.

Seabright, J. (2010). *So You Want to Be a Theatre Producer*. London: Nick Hearn Books.

Siegesmund, R., and Cahnmann-Taylor, M. (2007). *Arts-Based Research in Education: Foundations for Practice*. New York: Routledge.

Sinner, A., Leggo, C., Irewin, R., Gouzouasis, P., and Grauer, K. (2006). Arts-based education research dissertations: Reviewing the practices of new scholars. *Canadian Journal of Education*, 29(4), 1223–1270.

Smith, A. Deavere (1993). *Fires in the Mirror*. New York: Anchor Books/Doubleday.

Smith, A. Deavere (1994). *Twilight, LA. 1992*. New York: Anchor Books/Doubleday.

Solomon, A. (2001). Irony and deeper significance: Where are the plays? *Theatre 31*(3): 2–12.

Springgay, S., and Freedman, D. (Eds.) *Mothering a Bodied Curriculum: Emplacement, Desire, Affect*. Toronto, ON: University of Toronto Press.

Sykes, H., and Goldstein, T. (2004). From performed to performing Ethnography: Translating life history research into anti-homophobia curriculum for a teacher education program. *Teaching Education Journal*, *15*(1): 31–56.

Theatre Communications Group (2010). *Dramatists Sourcebook*. 26th edition. New York: Theatre Communications Group.

Trenka, J. Jeong. (2009). *Fugitive Visions: An Adoptee's Return to Korea*. St. Paul, MN: Borealis Books.

Trenka, J. Jeong. (2005). *The Language of Blood*. St. Paul, MN: Borealis Books.

Trenka, J. Jeong, Oparah, J. Chinyere, and Sun,Yung Shin (Eds.) (2006). *Outsiders Within: Writing on Transracial Adoption*. Cambridge, MA: South End Press.

Turner Strong, P. (2001) To forget their tongue, their name, and their whole relation. In: S. Franklin and S. McKinnon (Eds.), *Relative Values: Reconfiguring Kinship Studies* (pp. 468–93). Durham and London: Duke University Press.

Volkman, T. A. (2003). Introduction: Transnational Adoption. *Social Text 21*(1): 1–5.

Vonk, E. (2001). Cultural Competence for Transracial Adoptive Parents. *Social Work* 46(3): 246–255.

Wake, C. (2010). Verbatim theatre within a spectrum of practices. In P. Brown (Ed.). *Verbatim: Staging Memory and Community* (pp. 6–8). Strawberry Hills, NWS: Currency Press.

Wallis, L. (2005). *In Good Company: A Manual for Producing Independent Theatre*. Sydney: Currency Press.

INDEX

A